The Size of One's Paw

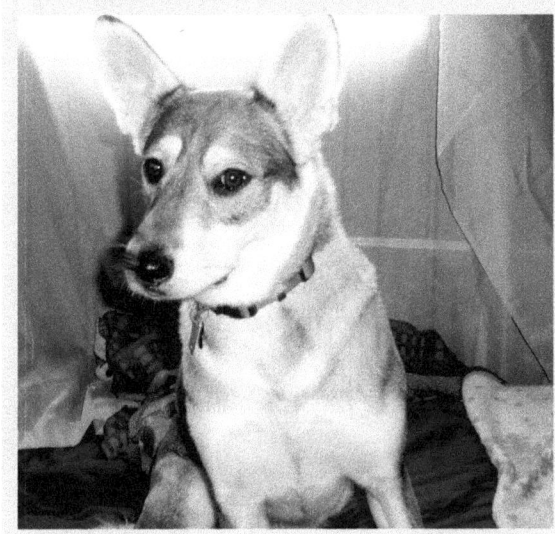

...has nothing to do with the size of one's heart

Nicole Tatara

DEDICATION

I dedicate this book to my daughter. She has shown me through her eyes that the world is beautiful, mystical, and surprising. I would like to humbly thank everyone whom has worked with my daughter since her birth (teachers, TSS, BSC, and all other staff whom have helped through the years). I whole-heartedly believe these individuals along with myself, my parents, and other close relatives and friends have all made a valuable impact on her life. Thank you!

Contents: Page:

Introductions

Baby Girl

When my husband, daughter and I were first looking for a dog we wanted to get a puppy. We had searched our local newspaper and Humane Society with limited success. None of the dogs or breeds listed seemed to spark our interest. We had searched regionally on Craigslist and found an ad for a CKC (Continental Kennel Club) Siberian Husky puppy. The picture was beyond adorable and an affordable price listed as fifty dollars. I have never had a Husky before, or a pure bred dog for that matter. The thought of it was appealing.

After speaking to the owner we left our rural home and headed for the city, Pittsburgh. It was a forty-five minute drive south, which was not bad by any means, but we were cautious when we found the address and pulled up. The neighborhood was not the best, but probably not the worst. I had not grown up in a large city and only have been briefly to a few of them; they are not always my favorite places. We parked and crossed the street to find the owner standing in the small fenced front yard with the Husky in his company. At first glance she was tall and too thin looking. She had lots of energy and happily greeted us despite her being slightly underweight. The introductions were all made and we went inside.

The family was inside with two dogs, including the Husky, four cats, and a large amount of reptiles. The owner said he was big into reptile shows. Personally, I never heard of a reptile show. Jason seemed more interested in the snakes, turtles, and creepy crawlies and mostly left the decision of the puppy up to Amber and myself.

I chatted with the wife about the Husky, who was originally named Sasha. Amber and I loved playing with her. She was bright and bouncy with affection and took to us

1

instantly. Jason and the owner disappeared into the basement to look at the pythons. I just did what any perspective owner would do ask questions, interact, and observe. We all had our heart set on adopting Sasha and knew we made a good choice. Sasha loved to play with the cats the most. The wife explained about how they had gotten her, from a neighbor that abused her and some other puppies that were over there. It touched my heart even more. Upon observance of Sasha she did not have any adverse effects either mentally or physically from the abuse. Sasha was raised by cats and in turn had behavioral tendencies like one. I noticed more than once she played with a ball using her paws like a cat and pounced around a lot. She had preferred the cats versus the reptiles, which were not her companions of choice. After a short stay and monetary exchange we proudly left with our new puppy.

We were excited and well prepared for the arrival of our new puppy, but like anyone we had questions that would only be solved by time. How would we all get along? Will this new dog fit well into our life and our home? Besides all of the common questions that pet owners ask themselves we had a few additional ones. We were concerned about the history of abuse when she was young. Even though she had no outward physical or mental disabilities we still did not know if there was anything else for us to anticipate due to it. Taking Sasha in as our own presented itself a risk. The only odd behaviors that we noticed was her shyness and her cat-like behavior. Everyone like's cat nip, don't they?

The arrival home meant big changes for us and a name change for Sasha. We decided that name would be no more. She was now Baby Girl, our baby girl. The family of three became a family of four that afternoon.

That weekend was warm and bright and we wanted to take our new puppy for a walk. The afternoon heat of a summer's day in rural western Pennsylvania provides a beautiful landscape with thick plush woods and long winding trails perfect for walking, riding, or hiking. The North Country Trail, which was made famous by George Washington, was located just north of our home, as well as other nearby nature trails. Our family enjoyed the outdoors and spent every last second we could outside.

The summer that we got Baby Girl, Jason had also gotten another baby girl. Except the other baby girl was not a dog, it was his Yamaha dirt bike, a TTRX 230. He rode in fields, trails, dirt roads, and mud pits.

"The muddier the better" he would always say.

Myself, Amber, and Baby Girl preferred to walk rather than ride as we did not care for mud, or so I thought. Jason had no fear. The dare-devil in him would never be repressed as long as the mud was not in short supply.

One particular late summer afternoon we went for a walk, while Jason rode. The air was warm, with a few wispy clouds, but mainly sunny skies. We trekked through the large field behind our house to the woods. The trails behind our property totaled thirteen and varied in terrain. I walked Baby Girl with leash in hand, or you could say that she had walked me. At six months in age she was strong and training her would to be a challenge. Amber took along with her a small portable container to catch bugs and she skipped, sang, and sprinted like any carefree child would. Jason rode his dirt bike; he'd dart ahead sometimes hitting third gear then would ride back to where we were. He most certainly left us in the dust, but always came back.

The forest was dense in some spots with very little sun hitting the ground. These were Jason's favorite spots;

3

these were the mud pits. He loved revving up the bike and riding through creating a fountain of mud. When we came up to the muddy spot Amber was thrilled. She had never seen so much mud in her life. She watched in wonder as Jason rode the bike through flinging mud everywhere. Baby Girl was equally thrilled with the flying mud and tried to catch a piece of mud as it flew towards her. I stayed clear of it as much as possible.

"Whoa! I want to try!" Amber exclaimed. "Daddy, can I ride with you?" She asked.

"It's ok with me, but you have to ask mom." Jason replied while taking off his helmet. A few times I nervously let Amber ride with Jason. The bike sat up high and was fast. The times that she did ride she had a helmet on and he went slower. This would be her first time going through a mud pit and I was concerned.

"I guess." I replied. Amber did a little dance and jumped once in excitement. I gave Jason a short lecture on safety with Amber on the bike like I always did. He was always careful, but I always did the motherly thing. Amber and Jason got prepped and I did my best to control Baby Girl. She wanted to play, to run, and to get muddy, but I did not.

Amber and Jason were on the bike and ready to go. I saw the anticipation grow in Baby Girl's expression. I had a bad feeling, not about them riding through the mud, but the ramifications that it would have on me. I stood back and off they went. The bike was only in second gear and I was worried about them slipping. I should have been worried about myself slipping as well. They hit the mud pit and mud went flying further and faster than the time before. Amber howled in delight and so did Baby Girl whom lunged and pulled. She ran and I fell.

It all happened so fast I could barely believe it. There Baby Girl stood above me licking the mud off of my face. She pulled so hard and the mud was slippery. I had landed on my rear end and was knee deep in the mud pit. The bike cleared the mud pit just fine; they stopped and were now turning around. I was in shock, both mad and laughing at the same time.

"Are you ok honey?!" He yelled as he came jogging over to me. I was still sitting there, horrified. Jason said he had never seen me like that before, mad and muddy.

"Here, let me help you up." He said with a slight smirk and took Baby Girl's leash and extended his arm and helped me up. Amber laughed. I was not amused, yet I laughed out of sheer embarrassment. Why would someone pay to go to a day spa when your dog can pull you through the mud pit behind your house for free?

Once up and on my feet I surveyed the damage. I had on tennis shoes, ankle socks, shorts, and a gray t-shirt all of which were drenched in mud. Jason and Amber barely had any mud on either one of them, only a little bit on their shoes and legs. Baby Girl had mud on her face, legs, and paws. She seemed to enjoy licking it off of her and me also. Now came the fun part, walking another two miles back to home. I have never wanted a shower so much in my life as it was eighty-five degrees outside and as I walked the mud began to harden.

The shock and anger quickly passed as we approached home. Jason rode very slowly beside us and occasionally took Baby Girl's leash which afforded me a break. Amber couldn't stop taking about how much fun mud was and she couldn't wait to do it again. She and I had varied ideas on the subject. Amber found a grasshopper on the way back which hitched a ride in the bug catcher. Later it was released in our backyard after she had shown the neighbors.

Jason was very understanding of the whole situation and didn't laugh, which helped me a great deal. Upon returning home I showered and had never appreciated soap as much as I did that day. Jason was grilling steaks and Amber played ball with Baby Girl. In all I did my best taking the incident with a grain-of-salt attitude and realized that almost anything can happen when you share your life, and your walks, with a dog.

Tazz

Puppy number two, another listing, and twice the trouble. "Free Puppies", the best things in life may be free, but come at a cost.

Christmas time that same year that we had adopted Baby Girl there had been an ad in the Butler Eagle and thought about getting another puppy. It was six months after we had gotten Baby Girl and thought that she was still young enough to accept another puppy into our household. Upon calling the owners, the pups were half Labrador Retriever and half German Shepherd. They had seven females and three males. We were excited and especially wanted a male dog this time. All family members agreed so we sent to see the free puppies.

This journey was more local than regional, and also more North, which was a blessing since it was December and Jason did not want to drive a long distance on icy roads unless it was necessary; snow is more accommodating than ice. The area was even more remote and rural than where we lived. There were winding hilly roads with scarce lights and signs; it took us a while to get where we were going.

We pulled up to a stately looking farm house in Butler County. I thought to myself *These people aren't hurting for money.* After the fact of bringing our puppy home Jason admitted thinking the same. There were large newer clean pickup trucks and fancy cars in the drive of the three story house. There was a wrap-around porch, garage, and pool in the backyard. We saw the mother dog, a yellow lab, tied to a running leash in the rear of the yard near a shed.

Jason, Amber, and I walked up the driveway to the side of the porch with the front light on. Amber asked to knock and did so pleasantly; she was trying her best to contain her excitement. A teenage boy and his mother answered the door. They came out with their coats on and the boy went to the shed to retrieve the pups. He made several trips carrying several dogs at a time. I talked with the mother about the puppies.

"They are seven weeks old and on solid puppy food." She reported.

A few of the puppies were on the porch now and Amber petted the few while we talked.

"Have they had their shots yet?" I asked as I picked up a beautiful yellow and white-colored female.

"No." The woman replied bluntly. "That's why they

7

are free. I didn't want to put much into them." The woman whom seemed pleasant at first now had a distain in her voice. She continued to explain that the mother dog was hers and a roving male German Shepherd had gotten into the yard and she wanted nothing to do with the puppies.

Now I was taken back with the whole situation, but kept my opinion to myself. All the puppies were finally brought out for us to look at and it did not take long to see that some of these puppies were not cared for properly. Some looked malnourished, some had a skin condition where the fur on the tail was gone, and a few had ragged coats that smelled grotesque. All of the puppies were cold and shivering. They were being kept in the shed with no heat. Both Jason and I were upset at this since we were avid dog lovers and this was an unacceptable way to treat puppies, no matter what the reason.

After looking at the lot, most of the puppies hid under the patio furniture to keep warm, except for one puppy. He was mostly black with a little white and did not have a skin condition as far as we could tell. He did smell, especially his breath, but we tried to overlook that and paid attention to his behavior and demeanor. Jason instantly fell in love with him. He scooped him up in his big manly arms and held him close to his chest to keep him warm. Amber liked all of the puppies and wanted them all. I shared her enthusiasm and wanted more than one, but in the end we picked Jason's puppy. The teenage boy said his name was Brutus. Well, we knew we had to change his name. A *Brutus* really didn't fit in with us.

We made our choice and thanked the owner's profusely. We offered her money for the pup, but she would not accept it. She did have a kind heart as to wanting the puppies to go to good homes for Christmas. It was a mixed blessing of sorts. A part of me was more than thankful for the wonderful puppy and the other part of me wanted to turn her into the authorities for the way the puppies were treated.

Come to find out a few days later our new puppy was sick. He had a type of worm parasite and often had diarrhea and vomiting. He required immediate vet care and ran the risk of death from those parasites. The Humane Society was contacted about the dogs living conditions. In retrospect, Jason and I wished we had taken one of the female puppies as well so we could have done more to help. If all of the dogs were sick we hoped their new owners had gotten them the treatment and preventative vet care right away.

As we drove home that night with our new puppy Amber had busily thought of new name choices. Among the top three were Butch, Tommy, and Prince Charles. Jason and I frowned at all the names.

"Keep thinking Amber. Give it time. We need to find a name that is perfect for him and fits well with all of us." I said to her. It didn't take long to pick out the name. Upon arriving home Jason put Baby Girl in Amber's room and I brought the new puppy in so he could walk around the living room. He had since on the way home kept warm and stopped shivering. He had a playfulness about him that could not be ignored, literally. He was cute, strong, and immediately starting getting into things within minutes.

The three of us sat on the floor with him and the puppy played. He seemed to favor Jason the most. At one point the pup started to chase his tail around in a circle almost like he had discovered it for the first time. With this black blurry thing swirling around on the floor the perfect name popped into my head and I let it burst out.

9

"Tazz! We should call him Tazz, because he looks like a Tasmanian Devil!" I was excited about the name.
"Yes!" Both Jason and Amber simultaneously said, and we all agreed. Tazz.

It was a most fitting name for his personality. He was dark in color, had a strong sense of self, and most of all he's a whirlwind of trouble. So that night the family of four became a family of five.

We had helped Tazz and in return he had helped us. At the ripe young age of eleven weeks old I knew he was a remarkable dog, for so many reasons. This moment in particular his nose had said it all.

Jason had a reoccurring eye infection and sties for several months. One had cleared up just prior of us getting Tazz, yet about a month after we had adopted him another one flared up. Jason had an especially awful time with this occurrence. Antibiotics proved not to help much and vision blurriness came and went often. Despite different medications, ointments, and home remedies the condition prevailed.

Jason and I were sitting on the couch one Saturday afternoon discussing work and our weekend plans. Tazz began acting out of the ordinary towards Jason. He nervously and compellingly kept licking Jason's left eye. Jason would push Tazz off and away from him in protest. This did not deter our puppy one bit and he only licked the left eye; paying no attention to the right one whatsoever. He was persistent on not giving up. We were astonished that Tazz knew how much the sty was bothering him. Tazz knew there was a problem and tried to remedy it the only way he knew how.

Within a few minutes Jason got up and went to the bathroom to put the medicated ointment in his eye. He was overdue for the dose and thought it may put Tazz at ease. I prepared a warm cloth for him and Jason put the ointment in and went to lie down. Tazz was on edge the whole time and seemed to relax when Jason did. While his intentions were to comply with Tazz's demands, Jason had helped himself considerably. He had felt a relief which affected both him and Tazz. Jason wondered if perhaps Tazz could sense it the relief that he was feeling.

Dogs are able to pick up on the slightest things that people cannot. We were amazed and perplexed that Tazz could accomplish this at such a young age. He recognized exactly where the trouble spot was and brought it to our attention. A dog's sense of smell is useful in so many areas to help mankind from cancer sniffing canines to tracking dogs. We know that we are truly blessed with an intelligent and compassionate canine.

Maxwell & Elliott

When you walk through Kyle and Denise's house, my parents, you need to watch where you step and sit for that matter. No blanket is safe or unoccupied. Maxwell, their three-year old beagle and basset hound mix has an obsession for comfort.

By fluffing, he tosses the blankets up in the air in and swirls them around. All you can see is a blur of black, white, and brown among the blanket as he contours it into the desired shape. He does this with a swift pre-planned spider-likeness that being the deliberate final product is of the utmost comfort. With his perfect pile of fresh fluffiness he dives in and buries himself into his cocoon. There is no visible sight of Maxwell. He must have an air pocket in there somewhere, else how could he breathe? I still wonder about that.

Maxwell often reminds me of Underdog. This mild-mannered beagle sits, stays, and lies around as any other dog would, but when the opportunity arises he breaks free from his tranquil shell and bursts into a fast frenzy of fresh activity.

No sheet, comforter, or blanket is safe in this house. So everyone watches and waits for the fluffing, it never fails to be a laugh out loud moment when it occurs. The rule of thumb before you sit down or get into bed is to check the blankets before settling in too comfortably.

Max is a unique dog with his unsurpassed motives for comfort. From the fur on his head to his white-tipped tail his soft fur is equivalent to the softness of his blankets. His favorite blanky is my mother's green, tan, and gray velvet comforter.

I've never been one for frivolous spending, but I cannot help myself looking through the Sunday newspaper advertisements for that one perfect comforter to fix Max's taste. I often feel like a teenager again when I go shopping at the mall. However, I am no longer sixteen years old and buying CD's or trendy clothes instead I am window shopping for Max. Occasionally that one perfect sale will give light to that one perfect blanket which catches my eye, and Max's taste.

Everyone has their icons, items, taboos, and limits when it comes to their dogs. I view myself as a liberal in my thoughts, a conservative to traditions, and a free-spirit when it comes to my dogs. There are active dogs, cute dogs, overweight dogs, and passive dogs along with dozens of other types. Maxwell is a passive dog by nature and is very selective among his breed at his best. He is an individual canine whom is choosy about his people and his pastimes, the blanket collection.

The sky and horizon are limitless spaces when it comes to how much space one dog can fill your heart with. We have Max's heart and he has ours, and our blankets.

Another canine family member is Elliott. He resides in northwestern New York State, just north or Buffalo and lives my brother and his family. We live three hours from each other and usually only get to see each other at holidays and other special occasions. Each visit includes the mingling of all of our dogs. The four-year old little Yorkshire Terrier, Elliott, always steals away our hearts with his cute little face and even cuter attitude.

This pup is compact and travel size, literally. Though he is only a mere five pounds in weight he travels heavily. His entourage consists of his people, Kyle and Bret, and two bags filled with all of his necessities. Food, distilled bottle water, toys, treats, and chewies are among those necessities. Not to mention his outfits. Elliott has a passion for fashion and loves to strut his stuff. He dons everything from a teeny Santa outfit at Christmas to a black leather biker jacket with rhinestone collar, and of course his olive-green tweed overcoat with matching fleece parka. He looks fabulous and proudly wears them all!

Yorkies are very discriminating dogs by nature. Their choice in companionship, food, and fashion sense are seemingly hard-wired into them. They are often the breed who wins best in show at AKC dog shows for the toy group. Elliott is not a "show dog" per se, yet he has the standard dark-steel blue coat and winning attitude and would surely take first prize. Bret and Kyle are devoted to their little pup in every way. They put a tremendous amount of work into Elliott's coat and care. A common saying "dogs resemble their owners" is no more true for Elliott, Kyle, and Bret.

Elliott is a key member at all the family functions. He seizes these moments with his showmanship and his flare. He is one dog who proudly displays real self with his undefined sense of self. This is a true expression without societal limits and conventions. Elliott and his people are true New Yorkers.

Milo

Most dog lovers started somewhere. Jason was fourteen years old when his family had gotten a Great Dane. In turn, the Great Dane had turned out to be the breed that influenced him the most. A family friend had given Jason's father and his step-mother a two-year old female Great Dane, Princess.

Princess was of the German Breed Standard of Great Danes. She was Harlequin in color being that the traditional white coat with black patches. She was regal in her beauty but was not trained as a dog should have been. When the Saunders's took her in she was housebroken, and followed only a few simple commands, but lacked in discipline and consistent training.

After a few short weeks they noticed that Princess was eating more and was more protective of herself and grew ever cautious of her surroundings. They suspected that she was pregnant and the vet had confirmed this. This was unexpected and more than what the family had bargained for when they accepted the free dog.

Soon enough the puppies were born. The plan was that they were going to keep Princess and Jason and his father would both pick one puppy each to keep. The litter consisted of fifteen puppies in all. Jason had first pick. He chose the first born pup, a male. He named him Milo. Milo was the largest and most healthy looking of all the puppies born. He wanted a dog that was tough and strong-willed just like he was. Jason Sr., in contrast, had picked the runt of the litter and named him Jack.

Eventually the other thirteen puppies needed a home. Jason's step-mother's father came over one day, Bobby, and was going to give the pups away. The pups were loaded into a box that said on the side. "Free To Good Home." Bobby took the box out to curbside of the main road. Jason figured that it wouldn't take long until all the pups had new owners. To Jason's surprise Bobby had returned back rather quickly with an empty box. Bobby was quick to avoid questions.

"It's all done." He told Jason. The entire situation was questionable, but Jason was happy to have Milo and to him that was the most relevant outcome that this possible disastrous situation had evolved into.

Milo was a magnificent Brindle color having a light golden fawn coat with black stripes that were his most defining feature. As a puppy he had a good temperament. He was energetic, excitable, playful, and he knew who his master was. Jason taught him as much as he could and took him almost everywhere he possibly could. Their favorite places to go together were the woods and various fishing spots. When Milo was a few months old the family moved and bought property on five acres of wooded land with a pond. Milo was in wide-open-space heaven.

Milo became more protective of Jason and his tough side was showing through with age. The pair often walked in the woods behind his home and on one afternoon walk when Milo was nine months old he smelled something in the woods that was not right. Jason recalled how Milo stopped and would try to block him from going any further. Milo was cautious and turned back and Jason followed him. He figured an animal was in the woods and Milo did not want Jason to continue. A few hours later in the backyard Milo started acting odd again and it was a good thing that he was on his running leash because three black bears walked along the tree line of the property. It was a mother and two cubs. Jason now understood what Milo was trying to say and do and he was very grateful.

Milo knew his perimeter and the yard was a battle field of sorts. Milo often caught ground hogs alive and brought them to Jason. He was proud of the seized intruders he caught and he wanted his master to know that. Milo was a protector, soldier, and executioner. No ground hog or any small animal was safe. One day a cat had unfortunately decided to eat out of Milo's food bowl in his dog house and that was the cat's last meal.

Jason had often thought of putting up a sign that read. "Warning – Doom to all groundhogs!" The words rang true and each groundhog paid as its predecessors did.

Milo was three years old when he knew something was wrong with Jason even before he did. Milo would act oddly around him and mellow out to some extent. He constantly snuggled with Jason and became even more protective of him. Jason soon after found out that he had kidney cancer. Jason's family was supportive as did the best they could, but Milo was Jason's companion and confidant through the entire cancer ordeal. From the first test and diagnosis through procedures, surgeries, chemo, radiation and finally remission; the entire journey had taken a year.

This time in Jason's life was exhausting and terrifying and Milo was the one who licked his wounds. Jason is ever grateful for Milo's unending caring and support. He was an unexpected puppy who exceeded all of Jason's hopes, dreams, and expectations.

Over time Jason's Milo went from being unexpected to unstoppable in so many ways. Jason transitioned from adolescence to adulthood with Milo faithfully at his side. He grew into a towering Great Dane. Jason was a rather tall man himself being six-foot and five inches tall, but when Milo stood on his hind legs and put his paws on Jason's shoulders he reached six-foot and eight inches tall. They were both tall and sturdy individuals with big prides and big hearts.

Milo grew ever more leery of those groundhogs. One day he had noticed something in the yard, near the pond, that he had never seen before and was curious. He brought it to Jason like all of the other small creatures, but instead of killing this one he seemed to nuzzle it which was heart warming to Jason. It was a baby yellow Canadian goose.

"Aww!" Jason exclaimed. "It's so small." He scooped the small yellow ball of fuzz in his hands while Milo watched with concern.

"You wanna keep him boy?" Jason asked with certainty.

They kept the gosling and Milo was its adoptive mother. Jason rigged up a heating lamp and pseudo nesting area for the gosling and they named him Quackie. Quackie was raised by Milo. He was a goose who tried to bark, but it came out as a long and winded quack. He acted like a dog and liked chewies and going after the groundhogs just like Milo. The egg does not fall far from the tree.

Quackie had a make shift nest just outside of Milo's dog house. He often slept there, but just like any other Canadian goose he loved the water and the Saunders's pond was just the right size. Jason's favorite past time was fishing. He did keep and eat some of the fish that he caught once in a while, but since they owned the pond Jason liked to stock it, especially with catfish.

Catfish are bottom feeding fish with long whiskers, boney fins, and sharp teeth, but in the pond they grew to be quite large. Quackie would go after some of the smaller and not quite so intelligent fish, but was careful not to sit in the water at night when the catfish were more active. Though Milo loved the water and swimming he soon learned that this pond was filled with fast-moving biting creatures and though he was tough, he was also smart enough to avoid it.

Though Milo had a soft spot for Quackie and Jason he disliked everyone else. He did not even care for Jason Senior or Jack. Jason was the only one Milo would allow to give him his food and water. Whenever one of Jason's friends, girl friends, or anyone came near the property Milo was on red alert mode. He barked, growled, and protected his owner to his best extent. Nothing or no one would come between him and his master. He was there for him through the worst moments of Jason's life. This is one Great Dane who's heart and loyalty was unsurpassed and unstoppable.

Searches and Rescues

One Powerful Sniffer

A dog's sense of smell is unbelievably stronger than a human's sense of smell. One of the dogs that I previously owned was a Black Labrador whom I trained for search and rescue. His name was Rocky. When he was full grown he weighed seventy-five pounds and which consisted of pure muscle. He was also mixed with Rottweiler which made his physique even more stocky, yet strong.

I began Rocky's basic obedience training when he was six months old. The class was held at a local kennel. It was close to my residence with an excellent reputation for obedience training. The trainer, Trish, was very much into the humane and holistic care for canines and horses alike. It took Rocky a while to get the hang of the obedience training. Trish often joked that my dog had ADHD. This forthcoming comment was not funny at the time, but true, and in retrospect proved to be a motivator. The other dogs in the class progressed faster than Rocky, but he and I stuck in there despite being outlanders.

The class was very structured and lasted for three months, three days a week, to be precise. It was cumbersome at times, but I was determined to have Rocky succeed. There were take home handouts and quizzes on both techniques and nutrition. In addition to the class time it was recommended that we practice the skills every day for at least fifteen minutes. The techniques worked over time using a combination of both voice and hand signals. The objective of each lesson was for the dog to know that the handler is in charge and they are to listen and follow commands.

The rewards used started out being small bits of food. Treats, cooked chicken, white cheese, and hot dogs were among the most common used. Eventually the food rewards were discontinued and the dog uses praise from their trainer as their reward. The program worked wonderfully. Despite the time and extreme effort put in Rocky and I had passed. The final and hardest task for the dog to learn is to sit in one spot while the trainer leaves the room. The dog is not supposed to move for two minutes. This was a challenge for Rocky to obtain, but after time and training he was able to do it.

We passed basic obedience class; we were thrilled!

After that I considered enrolling into an advanced obedience class, but instead had done it self-taught. Finding information from reference books and the internet I had continued on my own with training. From this Rocky had become a very smart and obedient dog.

A few months after the basic training had ended I decided to look into using Rocky for search and rescue. I had been a volunteer in a fire department for a few years and a neighboring department had a certified SAR dog and handler. Upon making contacts and researching I had decided that this was something that I wanted Rocky and I to do.

The county had a SAR team of canines as well. Due to political problems they were slowly disbanding and losing members. Most of these members had started their own SAR team. It was this newly-formed team that Rocky and I were involved in. The captain of the team, Bill, was the member at the neighboring fire department. The team consisted of handlers and their dogs. It began with four certified members and had taken on us as well for training. After an additional eighteen months of training Rocky was a certified search and rescue canine. The team had continued to expand taking on and training new members and their dogs.

The breeds that were on the team were Rottweilers, Blood Hounds, Labrador Retrievers, and German Shepherds. From start to finish Rocky was on the team for four years. He had completed many searches and found many lost people. The amount of missing or lost people in Erie County, PA that the team was called to varied anywhere from a few per year to a dozen per year. Less was always better for the missing persons, but not beneficial for the canine's skill set.

The team trained at least once a week, and sometimes twice a week. The handlers would bring friends or family to help out and be pseudo victims. I myself had been a "victim". It is not an easy task. It involves being out in all types of weather and often being in the woods for an extended period of time. Bugs, ticks, spiders, swamps, heat exhaustion, and the occasional frost-bitten toe was all part of the experience of being the lost victim.

Scent discrimination is the main component to how canine search and rescue is accomplished. The pseudo victim leaves a scent article that has exclusively been worn by the victim; usually a hat, glove, or other article of clothing works best. The dogs and handlers are kept out of sight from the victim. The victim leaves the scent article on the ground and walks towards the hiding spot. We often used different densely wooded areas for the training searches to occur. After the pseudo victim was in route the dogs would sniff the scent article and their handlers would signal to their canine for the search to begin.

A handler with their dog would go first, one pair at a time. The handler would use a specific set of commands for the canine during the search. The dog would go up to the search article and smell it for a minute or so, taking in the human's scent from the article. Then the handler and dog were off. The handler is not to influence the dogs while tracking. They simply held the leash and were guided, sometimes running while being guided if the dog caught the scent really strong. Most of the time, the dogs would find the victim. Often the victims tried to make the search complicated to give the dogs more of a challenge.

The scent article contains thousands of dead skin cells from the missing person. When the canine smells the article they are looking for that particular scent. The specific smell that the dog actually follows is that of the specific DNA of that person. Those cells give off a gaseous byproduct, or waste. The dog follows the gaseous waste smell from the trail that the person leaves as they walk and move around. The dead skin cells fall off of a person's body constantly. In fact, the only way a dog is not able to smell these cells if a person was in a completely air tight suit, such as a spacesuit.

The perfect condition for the canine to follow the scent is in a dewy wet grass. The DNA gaseous waste clumps together on the wetness and stays on the grass and is not inclined to move very much. The scent is more constrained and is easier for the dog to pickup and follow. By contrast, scenting for DNA during and/or after falling snow is harder for the dogs. A human perspective would think that the tracks have been covered up, but to the canine the scent is covered up and what remains of the scent lays on top of the snow and the air or wind swirls the scent around. It is harder for the dog to track, but it is not impossible.

Most dog breeds do air scenting in which the scent is hanging and suspended in the air. An air scenting dog will have his or her head up while they track. The Blood Hound breed is very effective at the opposite, they sniff the ground. Their long ears are made to swing across the ground and kick up the scent to their nose. This is why Blood Hounds are often seen with their heads to the ground while tracking.

As training continues the dog refines his skills and can pick up harder scents than the amateur canine. The handler refines his or her skills by methodically using commands and learns the body language of the dog. When a dog is picking up on a strong scent the handler must be able to recognize this. The dog will typically run and will seem more excited. The dog basically gets into his own world and has tunnel vision. When a victim is found the dog is trained to go up to the victim and turn right around and go to the trainer and stop. The search is over for the dog as he has accomplished his task.

The handler now takes over and a lot of praise is given to the canine. In both training and real searches portable two-way radios are used. In a real-life search the handler and canine that finds the victim may be separated from the rest of the search group. If the wind is strong the scent can be carried off in various directions and takes the canines with them. With the use of radios the handler who reaches the victim first will radio in that the search is over and give the location of the victim. The handler and dog both stay with the victim until help arrives.

Often these real-life searches involve several agencies such as ambulance crews, EMTs, firemen trained in rescue, police, and other volunteers. If the victim is hurt, and/or depending on weather conditions the handler may need to provide emergency medical care. Most canine handlers are some variance of EMT, paramedic, or first responder. A handler should have a first aid kit, water, and various supplies on him or her. The more prepared the handler is, the better off they will be as well as the victim.

The real heroes of search and rescue are the canines. These dogs go through long, tedious, and constant training in preparation for the real event. These types of organizations are usually volunteers and would not be possible without the selfless people who put in the time, energy, money, and their hearts into it. Without these dogs and their extraordinary sniffing ability it would make finding lost or missing people more difficult. I have been blessed to be a part of the SAR experience and have the utmost respect for the canines and the handlers who participate and train endlessly. They provide a valued and great public service.

The Gentle Giant

Saint Bernards are a ruefully large breed of canine. They have an oversized heart to go along with their extravagant size. They have also been kept in good company since the tenth century. The breed originated in the Alps in Switzerland at the Hospice of St. Bernard.

Travelers would migrate through the mountain pass to the border if Italy. It was often a peril less journey. Most often the weather conditions were wintry and travels faced extreme cold and danger. The Catholics and Monks frequented the Hospice and recognized a need to train the Saint Bernards to rescue the stranded travelers.

Saint Bernards still are bred and raised at the Hospice and typically twelve or more dogs reside there at any given point in time and are trained in rescue. The training of these canines for rescue takes approximately two years. As a continuing tradition these dogs would leave Hospice every morning and travel the mountain pass looking for travelers who need rescued from the snow and wintry conditions.

One of the most famous and unsurpassed Saint Bernards at Hospice was Old Barry. In his twelve years he had rescued over forty people. The rescue training ability is characteristic of the Saint Bernard breed and after the breed was started in Switzerland the breeding then spread to Germany and England. From countries to continents the majestic breed had spread. The 1960's was the decade when the Saint Bernard finally came to North America. By 1962 the AKC had more than 2,400 registrations consisting both of smooth-coats and rough-coats. Several SBCA (Saint Bernard Club Associations) had started through out the United States; they became established and were rapidly accepting members.

Continuing on with the reputation as a working dog Saint Bernards soon found their place in the United States doing rescue work as well. "They have a highly developed sense of smell and also seem to have a sixth sense about impending danger from storms and avalanches." These canines proudly and effectively do their search and rescue in the Rocky Mountains. The breed's incredible strength and size affords these canines to pull the victims out of the snow with ease. A male Saint Bernard weighs between one-hundred ten pounds to one-hundred eighty pounds and females generally weigh slightly less.

Saint Bernards are one of Jason's favorite breeds. He was born in Salt Lake City, UT and lived there until the age of five. When he was a toddler he and his father were driving on

a dirt road on the side of a mountain when a small yet sudden avalanche occurred. The car was covered with four to five feet of snow extending above the car. The car was pushed up against a guard rail, but thankfully did not go over the side of the mountain, yet the car would not budge. Jason's father, Jason Senior, tried to escape, but the weight of the snow proved to be too much.

They were trapped for a couple of hours. Finally, a SAR team consisting of a dozen members and two Saint Bernards had found the covered car. Jason Sr. recalls hearing the faint voices of people and the first thing he saw when they were discovered was a large tan and white face covered in snow and drool. After the vehicle was discovered all of the volunteers got busy shoveling and digging out the side doors of the vehicle. Before he knew it they were out of the car and a medical team was checking over the father and son.

They were both cold, but luckily they were unscathed. Jason Senior did not want to go to the hospital, but they were taking Jason Jr. as a precaution since he was so young and exposed to the cold. Thankfully, they were both fine and rescued quickly. Both Saint Bernards which led the team were males and both had fluorescent yellow dog vests on with *Red Cross* symbols on the vests.

The Saunders's rescue would not have happened as quickly as it did without the keen smelling sense and compassion of the Saint Bernards. They have the natural built-in skills hard-wired and passed down from centuries which when paired with specialized SAR personnel provide a much needed service to trapped and/or injured persons. The team members rely on the Saint Bernards to lead the way

26

and the key to their success is in the human-canine duo. Persons worldwide require this type of rescue effort and it is provided by the most capable and colossal members of the team, the Saint Bernard.

The Unanticipated Deliverance

Newfoundlands have been known for and specifically bred for water rescues. They have also been avid ship dogs and being in the working class of canines they have scaled up to that reputation. Most have anyways; this is not the case for Persey, a black and white four-year old female Newfoundland. The closest thing that Persey had ever come to being a water dog is getting bathed at the groomers. This was fine with Persey, she got lots of exercise with her owner, Elizabeth, whom took her for long walks every afternoon. The advantage to walking over water exercise is that there is no "wet dog" smell.

Persey might as well been a toy breed as she was spoiled and pampered and she did not seem to fit in well with the "working class" of canines. There was a nearby lake and creek, but her family hardly ever took her swimming or near the water. Elizabeth, from her childhood, had an expressed fear of the water. Her husband Brian was the opposite. He played water polo in college and loved to swim. Their son, Joey, had taken some swimming lessons and had become more interested in water sports as time progressed.

The Cadmore family was half and half. The women preferred to stay on land while the men were in the water.

The Cadmores were the same as any other middle-class American family. They had a modest house in a subdivision, were married, and had a child and a dog. Brian was a production supervisor at a plastic manufacturer while Elizabeth worked part-time as a columnist at a newspaper. Joey was in finishing up middle school, being at the end of his eighth grade year, and was off to high school that fall. He played basketball in middle school, but now his interest in water sports were at their peak. He planned on trying out for the swim team and water polo team. This made his father happy and his mother extremely worried.

Joey's best friend Mike was interested in the swim team and also kayaking and his other friend Sam was trying out for the water polo team and track and field. Mike's older brother and sister were both part of a kayaking team. The team met every Wednesday evening at the nearby creek. Joey was most especially excited with the thought of kayaking. He had seen it done a few times, not just on tv, but also in person. He and his friends liked watching the team. They came, assembled, geared up, and took off down the creek.

The creek, Boulder Creek, was part of a state park just six miles from the Cadmore's house. It was named Boulder Creek from all the large boulders and rock formations that a glacier had created and left behind during the last ice age. One portion of the park had a rock-climbing area where the three-hundred foot drop was appealing to some. There was also an old, but passable, covered bridge, an old mill, and two other bridges: Breakneck and Eckert. The thought of Breakneck Bridge put chills down Elizabeth's spine and she did nearly break her neck when she slipped partially down a mountain slope a few years prior.

The park was as beautiful as any landscape was ever made with Boulder Creek running right through the middle of it. Some areas are calm with sand and beaches and others were rapid. This is where the kayaking was at its best. Memorial Day weekend brought the pleasant thoughts of picnics, barbeques, and the warm air of summer seeping in. The Cadmore's plans were to picnic with Mike and Sam's family at the beach near the creek. Elizabeth agreed. She looked forward to the cool air and breezes, but disliked the thought that Joey would want to go swimming.

It was Memorial Day morning and Elizabeth had just finished whipping up the macaroni salad when the phone rang.

"Would you get that?!" She yelled to Joey whom was in the living room.

Joey was sitting on the dark apholstered couch playing his XBOX 360 with Persey sleeping next to him.

"Ok!" He yelled in reply and sprung off the couch to answer the phone. Persey was displeased at being interrupted of her nap and stretched her front legs out as far as they could go and relaxed. Joey said "Thanks. See you soon." He hung up and walked into the kitchen. Now his mom was frosting some cupcakes.

"That was Sam. He said that they are bringing their dogs also and said we can bring Persey if we want." Joey snagged a cupcake off the counter while Elizabeth had a perplexed look. *Why would we bring Persey? She can't swim.* She thought to herself as Joey gulped the last crumb down.

"I don't know." She hesitantly replied to Joey. "She can't swim for one and two..." Joey had cut her off.

"All dogs can swim mom." He bluntly countered her first comment as any teenager would. *Dogs are supposed to be natural swimmers.* The thought passed through her mind as Joey said it. "I looked up Newfoundlands and they are one of the best swimmers." He started going on about their history and Elizabeth knew she was going to be debunked on this one. *Darn internet.*

"Well, ask your father. If something happens I can't go in after her." Joey smiled. Of course dad was going to say yes.

Persey now got up and walked slowly into the kitchen. She knew they were talking about her and wanted to be in on the conversation. Joey had gotten the permission that he wanted from his father and being overjoyed he took Persey out in the backyard and tossed a tennis ball around. Persey jumped at the idea the walk was going to be

postponed because of the holiday, but no matter a ball was a fine replacement. Elizabeth finished packing the cooler when Brian walked in the room.

"You told Joey yes." She tried to keep her tone neutral.

"Yep. It's a good idea. Dog needs to learn how to swim." He also picked up a cupcake and in two bites it was gone.

"Ok. Just make sure they don't go in where it's too deep or rapid."

"Sure hun." He kissed her once softly.

"Thanks for the cupcake." Elizabeth lost this battle, but it didn't matter much. She had a good husband and son whom were sometimes too much alike. They acted similar and looked similar, both having light brown eyes and dark hair. Now though Joey's hair was two shades lighter from all the chlorine in the YMCA's pool.

It was almost noon and the Cadmore's arrived at the spot first. There was a sigh of relief that no one else had taken the beach spot. Multitudes of butterflies fluttered around which Persey went after right away. The three of them carried everything down the short trail to the sandy beach. There were several picnic tables, a permanently fixed charcoal grill, a large flat boulder on the right, a very tall towering bridge to their left, and shallow soft-running waters. All were happy with the spot that they had chosen. Soon after Sam arrived with his parents and his dog, Katy, whom was a Portuguese Water Dog. Their arrival was followed by Mike's family which included his parents, his two older kayaking siblings, and Rufus, a Curly-Coat Retriever. All together there were six adults, five teenagers, two water dogs, and a novice, a would-be water dog.

The picnic went off without a hitch. Everyone brought food and it was eaten up like there was no tomorrow. The dogs enjoyed the spread just as much as their human counterparts did. The three teen boys finished first. They were well prepared and had their swim suits underneath their shorts and were the first to go in the calm creek waters. They got prepped as did the dogs then like a flash the boys were off running towards the water with the dogs at their heels. The three friends were in anticipation of splashing in the cool water and looked forward to swimming and playing with their dogs. Pair by pair they splashed in. Joey was in the rear with Persey, whom halted the second her paws reached the water. Joey was in now and turned around and looked back.

"Come on girl!" Joey yelled.

Persey only stood there smelling the water and testing it very femininely with her front right paw. She was not going in. She looked up at Joey and whined before turning around and laying on the sand. Joey sighed with disappointment and continued in after his friends.

Elizabeth had seen all of this and was equally distraught. She was bothered with herself for having Joey and Persey life such a sheltered life. As a mother she tried to protect her son the best she could and now questioned her doubts. Joey had grown into a head-strong teenager and she knew that she had to start lightening up.

Persey laid in the sand watching for a few minutes and quietly moved to a nearby boulder. It was very large, flat, and stuck out into the water. She climbed up there and just laid there for a bit and watched the group play, laugh, and splash in the water. The kids found a shady area in the water where the waters were calm and there was plenty of shade. That afternoon headed up to a stifling eighty-nine degrees with high humidity. The adults felt every bit of it, but none of their children did. Persey had enough of lying around and being depressed. She jumped up and sat next to the adults; there she was in better spirits. She got a lot of attention and even more table scraps. Persey was petted and played with, but still kept a watchful eye on Joey in the water.

"Look here comes one!" Sam shouted to the group and pointed up-creek.

There was a kayaker maneuvering his way through the rapids and was descending now into the calmer waters. The set of rapids just above were small but still tricky. While going down the creek first there are a set of boulders on the right and then on the left and at the very bottom there was a small set of two whirlpools. Any rapid waters were not for novices no matter how easy. The red kayak with white pinstripes was now gliding with out assistance while the man had rested his arms for a minute while he glided slowly through the calmer waters.

The group of teens and their dogs were now on the side of the creek so the kayak could pass.

"Nice one man!" Mike had yelled.

"Thanks!" The kayaker had replied. As he neared the very calm waters under the large concrete bridge and passed the boys he began to paddle again, picking up in his pace. The boys were in awe and praised each other.

"That was awesome." Joey had said to Sam and high-fives were spread all around as the kayak disappeared from sight around a bend.

Out the three Mike was the only one who had got to try out a kayak. His older brother and sister occasionally let him paddle it in the calm shallow lake waters. They didn't dare let him try the creek yet. One minute the water is tranquil, but if the vessel gets into a certain range then you are off and Mike was nowhere being ready to attempt any kind of rapids.

Neither Sam nor Joey had ever sat in a kayak let alone paddle in one. They knew that it would not always be the case. *I can't wait to be on the kayaking team.* Joey had thought to himself.

In the passing moments Persey had gulped down charred pieces of hot dogs and left over hot dog bun crumbs. She was in heaven as far as she was concerned; she had her people, food, and plenty of attention. Elizabeth was relaxing on the picnic bench petting Persey and mentally had drifted off. She was thinking of a way to make it up to Joey. Looking around she had gotten several ideas for her column and she wanted Joey to be involved as well. *Outdoor sports, kayaking, swimming competitions...* thoughts were filling her head and she smiled at herself for the idea. Brian came over and hugged her which was followed by a back massage with Persey at their feet lying down. It was a most satisfying afternoon.

Elizabeth continued to think. *Maybe interviews with these types of athletes and participants? Joey would like that. It is definitely time to ease up.* She was deep in thought, letting her brain drift in and out. She was sublimely relaxed barely paying attention to the world around her when she suddenly snapped out of it to the sounds of screams.

The screams came from the panicky crowd from across the other side of the bridge. Elizabeth leaned forward to see what was going on. Persey's ears perked up as much as they could be while Brian and Sam's father ran up the trail and over to see what was going on. The three teens were out of the water and shouting and pointing up as well.

"Oh my God!" Elizabeth exclaimed and her hand went instinctively to her chest.

There was a young boy hanging from the south side pillar of the bridge dangling over the creek.

"What happened?" Brian asked as he neared the group where the boy was. He had been a lifeguard and member of the coast guard for many years and he appointed himself in charge as an uncle of the young boy's gave 911 the details.

"Chuck was here one minute and I looked around for him the next and he was up there; he must have climbed up." Chuck's father explained what had happened, he looked up worriedly and was visibly upset.

The boy had climbed up metal ladder spokes protruding from the cement pillar and had gotten stuck. He was hanging on for his life and screaming

"Help!" He yelled and panicked.

There was nearly a seventy-five foot drop which wasn't the worse of it. The best case scenario was he would land in the deep and calm water, but it was a stretch. The worst case was the more likely of the two being that if he fell he could hit the cement pillar on the way down or land on the boulder that was straight below him. Brian and a few of the adults organized a plan, but the women thought it was better to wait.

"It would take at least half an hour for a rescue group to arrive and the boy may not last that long." Brian addressed the group and they made up their minds. Persey had stayed on shore near Elizabeth and Joey was headed towards them with a towel draped over his shoulders.

"What's going to happen Mom?" Joey asked.

"I don't know. Your father's trying to help..." Her voice trailed off and she felt helpless. *He needs rescued, delivered from death.* She thought it, but kept it to herself. The crowd had grown both up above on the road and bridge and also down below hikers on the trail came over and even a few kayakers stopped and docked on the shore.

Persey stood near the two of them and was extremely upset. She paced and howled and protested the event the only way she knew how.

"I've never seen her like this." Joey had said to his mother.

"Me neither." She somberly replied. *Does she know something bad is happening?* Elizabeth questioned herself and decided without a doubt that *Yes,* Persey could sense how the people felt and was reacting appropriately. Persey was always sensitive to their emotions and was proud of her for being worried.

Brian and the small group of adult men went up after the boy and decided to perform a rescue by themselves. Elizabeth did not agree, but the decision was not hers. She could only do what she had always done, worry. It was the only thing that she was really good at. The men had gathered a large amount of blankets from their vehicles and set them on the boulder below the boy while ten men stood there waiting to catch him if needed. Brian, whom often liked being the hero, was the one with the most experience and courage, so he climbed the metal ladder and went up to retrieve the boy.

Brian was only a few feet off of the ground on the fifth rung when it happened. Persey perked her head up and ran with everything she had and dove into the water.

"What?" Joey and Elizabeth questioned. They looked up to see the boy falling. By the time the entire crowd had seen and comprehended the boy was nearly in the water. There was a loud splash when he went in just missing the boulder.

"Get him!" Brian yelled. Persey was on her way. She had never swum before and didn't even like getting her paws wet, but she had sensed the boy would fall in the second that it happened. Her senses and instincts did not fail her in this moment. The boy was unconscious yet floating and began drifting down stream.

"Oh God!" Chuck's mother screamed up on top of the bridge. Her mind could not keep up with seeing her son floating down the creek.

A few of the adults jumped off of the boulder and into the creek, but the water was getting more deep and rapid by the foot. Persey had swum past the adults and grabbed the child by the shirt near his shoulder and began paddling backwards. Mixed ooh's and aaww's came from the crowd as Persey swam hard and used all of her strength to make it back to the shore. Three adults were wading in the water near the shore. Persey instinctively got the boy and brought him to safety as he was delivered into their waiting arms. This was not Persey's usual character and it was shocking and unanticipated, but something in Persey had snapped and a century's worth of instincts flooded every part of her canine body. She didn't think and only acted upon it.

The boy was on shore yet still unconscious. Brian parting though the crowd and did CPR, he cleared Chuck's airway. He was alive and began vigorously coughing up water and was rolled on his left side. Chuck opened his eyes just as the ambulance and rescue crew arrived. He smiled and was happy to see his mom and dad standing above him. His mother cried and hugged him continuously he was then taken to the hospital for a broken arm. Chuck's father thanked the Cadmore's over and over and especially thanked Persey.

Persey was proclaimed a hero. Chuck and his family had visited often with the Cadmores and Persey was showed with attention after the rescue. There were television crews, reporters, and photographers, but Persey did not care much for the limelight and neither did his owners. Elizabeth of course got the only article exclusive on the rescue and kept the exposure to a minimum for her family's sake. Afterwards, she was appreciative in the turn of events and decided to lighten up on everyone - Brian, Joey, Persey, and herself.

Joey made the swim team and the water polo team at Boulder Creek High. Him, Mike, and Sam met with and watched the kayak team as often as they could, but they still had two more years until they could join. So much good came out the near dire event; the heroic action was unanticipated by all, yet Persey did what her ancestors had done for generations before her and she couldn't have done a better job if she had trained all of her life for that moment. When it came to Persey's water rescue skills, she had delivered them perfectly.

Icy Rescue

When Margo Vislecki was in her large yard on a cold March afternoon the last thing she expected to hear was a high-pitched bark coming from the north, near Spa Creek.

Margo and her husband Kent lived near Annapolis, MD and having property near the creek and just down from the marina was great for recreation, but now on this day brought a terribly fearful situation. The sounds of the panicking barking ahead of her in the direction of the creek held a meaning of possible disaster.

"Kent!" She yelled and hurried inside to retrieve her husband. Within minutes the pair had returned and Margo was calling 911. They were making their way down to the creek and the whimpering was louder and sounded more desperate.

For March there was surprisingly little accumulation of snow on the ground and trees, yet the temperatures were frigid when the wind blew strong. The creek had large patches of ice stuck to the banks and were also covered with snow.

A few small branches, also iced over, floated with the current intermittently on the icy temperate creek.

"Where is he? I don't see him." Margo was holding in the panic in she felt for the canine and scanned the banks for sight of him. She was on the line with a dispatcher and wanted to give a visual confirmation that for sure that there was a dog in the creek.

"There he is!" Kent pointed and yelled.

"Yes." She told the dispatcher. "There is dog in the creek. It looks like he is leaning against a down tree and near a large rock." Margo hurriedly gave their location and all the info that she could. "Please hurry." She pleaded and hung up. "They are on their way..." She sighed after her voice trailed off.

The mostly brown colored dog was against the fallen tree. The front part of his body slumped over the branches and he looked as if he was holding on for dear life. He continued whimpering and had his head down. There was a large rock which supported the tree and the dog was safe, for the moment. Margo prayed that the dog would be able to hold on until help arrived.

The pair could tell that he'd been through a lot; he looked as if his will had been sucked out of him and was drained from all energy and hope. He was obviously drenched from the water and patches of ice were visible on his fur. From across the creek all they could do was watch, this did not sit well with Kent.

"I have to do something." Kent spoke with a certainty that frightened Margo. She had known her husband all too well and knew that he would try to do something stupid.

"I'm going in and putting on my wet suit." He told her.

"Oh no your not. That water is freezing and you can't pull that dog out alone." She replied demandingly. Kent did what he needed to do. He went in and put on his wet suit and Margo watched the dog helplessly. All she could do was keep calm in this moment and try to stop her husband from going in the frigid water.

By the time Kent was returning the sirens could be heard faintly from the west. The first crews were in route and rapidly approaching their destination.

"Kent you're not going in." She sternly snapped.

"Well then they better hurry up. He's running out of energy and if he falls back in the water he may not be able to ever get out." Kent was pumped on adrenaline, but listened to his wife. He did not want to go in unless it was absolutely necessary. He wouldn't risk his life in the icy creek for an unknown dog unless it was the only option.

Margo had gone up to the drive to flag down the rescue crews. To their luck, help had arrived and there was no need for Kent to be the hero today. Kent was in excellent physical shape for being in his early forties. He was athletic and worked out whenever possible. He was a former fireman and rescuer. Today he would assist however possible, but was not going to risk his life for his family's sake.

A crew of five men approached with Margo at the lead.

"He's over there." She pointed and they picked up the pace.

"Ok. Let's get those ropes over there and tie up..."
The assistant chief started to give the orders to his crew
when he was interrupted by a loud cracking noise. The small
group stared over that the dog and the branch was splitting
and giving way.

"No!" Margo shouted and in the water the dog fell.
He was momentarily submerged before his head had popped
back up. He was treading water but losing energy fast. He
had let out a loud yelp and treaded faster.

Immediately the crew moved in unison and as fast as
possible. They futilely tossed out ropes with rescue devices
on the end in hopes the dog would bite or grab on to one of
them. This was not the case and the large brown dog went
floating down the creek like a piece of driftwood. He was
alive, but gone from sight.

The Assistant Chief had contacted dispatch and the
other crews. Option two was to set up a little bit further
down the creek and access the dog from there. The crew ran
with gear in their hands and on their backs and headed back
up to the driveway towards the trucks. The chief had directed
that if Margo and Kent wanted to come along they could
follow. That's just what they did.

The second crew was setting up a mile down the
creek. The water was more accessible, flowed slower, and
was more shallow here. The crowd was growing as well. All of
the sirens and apparatuses were attracting attention and
now the press was getting on scene. News crews and print
news crews were kept as far back as possible. Stand-by
ambulances arrived along with an animal control crew with
consisted of an ASPCA officer and a vet tech. The rescue

truck with the assistant chief pulled up second to last with Margo and Kent following. Everyone was ready and in place.

A white-hat officer was dealing with the press and all of their "breaking news" stories. She had explained the crucialness of getting the dog out on the first try at this point. Not only would the dog be water-logged and suffering from hypothermia, but another mile and a half down the creek was the junction to the Severn River. The river meant a larger body of faster moving water, and more rapids and currents. After the river, if the dog lived that long, meant Chesapeake Bay, and finally the Atlantic. The situation was dire and every effort was being made to rescue this dog.

The news report also consisted of a plea for the dog's owner to contact the police. They needed to know whom the dog belonged to and what had happened to him which ended up with the dog in the icy creek.

The news report had fallen on the owner's ignorant ears, but was recognized by the owner's neighbor, Vicki Ponson. Both the news crews' live feed and amateur videos were being televised and Vicki knew that dog. He was a German Pointer, brown with white and gray speckles around his muzzle, head, and neck. The crass old neighbor of hers was an alcoholic and abusive on his best days. Today must have been one of his bad days as she had not seen the dog at all today and now it was on television fighting for his life. There was no dog outside today, just a large pile of empty bottles accumulating at the back door.

"What did he do?" Vicki wondered and was outraged. She called the police.

The dog was half unconscious and partially laying on a piece of wood which kept his head out of the water. He was fast approaching the site.

"Here he comes!" One of the volunteers shouted and everyone got ready.

"No screwing up." The assistant chief thought. With thousands of people watching, the pressure was high enough already and the last thing he wanted was to add increasing stress to his men.

The German Pointer neared the second rescue site and the volunteers wading in the water. "This has to work." Several of the volunteers and members of the crowd were thinking, including Margo.

The closest dive team member to the dog had swum closer with rope in hand and plowed forward towards the dog. He missed. The next closest rescuer tried as well and failed. He lunged, but slipped on a mossy rock and fell in the creek. The surrounding volunteers helped the two men who had fallen and the dog continued to float by just out of their reach. None of the volunteers would let another one fall into the frigid water risking injury in order to save a dog. That was the truth.

Kent and Margo were just as disappointed as everyone else in the crowd when the petrified dog continued moving down the creek. The third checkpoint was also the last one before the river junction and these crews, almost a mile down, were in place and ready to go. The call came over the radio to command and to get set. Kent and Margo did not rush off to the third sight and just sat and watched the news coverage. There were plenty of other people rushing there and they would go when the dog was pulled out. They had a sense of duty to be there for the dog, yet they did not want to get in the way of the rescuers doing their jobs.

The third site had dozens of volunteers in the water this time, holding a large net. It was of tennis court quality being long and spanned across most of the creek. The water was more rapid here, and it was their last best option. Twenty men and women stretched across holding the net standing in the creek at foot-long intervals. Likewise, another dozen stood behind them for support. More than likely when the large dog would slam into the net a few volunteers, at minimum, would fall and be dragged into the water as well. It was their last safe attempt.

Margo prayed that the dog would be alright. Instead of her being there first hand on the scene, now she was an observer there watching the television. She was thankful that their three kids were not there to witness this event; they were at their grandparents for the weekend. She was sure that the kids, or at least her parents, were seeing this unfold on tv or hearing about it on the radio. Despite the grim situation she smiled inwardly and thought. "We've always wanted a dog."

"Kent lets go down there." Margo said to her husband.

"But he's almost there and we're going to miss it." He replied not really wanted to go down there and be amongst the chaos.

"I know, but I have a feeling and we've been here from the beginning and I think we should be there when the dog is brought in." Kent knew there was no point in arguing with her. They headed down toward the site.

The volunteers braced themselves for the impact. The water was much more rapid here and he was picking up speed despite his efforts to tread water in the opposite direction. "Here we go!" One of the male rescuers yelled just seconds before the dog crashed into the net. He directly hit one woman volunteer who had fallen sequentially. In the moments following four other volunteers were pulled and fell as well. The rear line of men and women came up instantly to help their fallen.

The dog's position held strong with the help of everyone. Moving as one they pulled the panicky dog to the shore line. The crowd watched breathlessly and did not make a sound until the dog and all the volunteers were safely on land.

"Yeah!" A loud and simultaneous roar emanated from the crowd and spread to all the volunteers. Praises and high-fives were given and passed around. The news reporters repeated the footage eagerly over and over and told the story of the heroics and rescue attempts of the ice-covered canine.

As soon as the dog was brought up on shore he was immediately turned over to the vet squad. The animal control team was joined by onlookers consisting of veterinarians and vet techs who wanted to help the distraught canine. Most waited with blankets. The dog's vitals were checked and despite everything his overall health was stable. The dog suffered from slight hypothermia and the frozen ice in his matted hair was being to melt from the warm temp of the van. He was no longer panicky, but was limp from exhaustion and laid there while several people tended to him at once. It was bliss compared to being in the creek. He wore no collar; his unofficial name was chocolate because of his dark fur.

Likewise the EMS rehab unit had tended to volunteers. Some needed gauze and bandages, but all were wet and needed warmth. Luckily no one had any serious injuries.

The assistant chief came over to check on the status of the rescued dog. He smiled eagerly through his robust facial expression carrying his gut.

"How's he doing?" He asked attentively.

"Surprisingly good considering." One of the vets answered him. "His fur is really matted and he's cold, but he'll pull through fine. I wish we could find out what happened." She replied. Margo and Kent were there and had seen the crews pull the German Pointer out of the creek. They watched the vets work on him, but kept a distance and didn't say much.

"That's another reason I came over here. We got the guy who did this. Turns out his neighbor was watching and recognized the dog. She'd hadn't seen it all day and called the police. The owner was intoxicated when the squad car went to check out the situation. It turns out that he was drunk this morning, almost all mornings, and he got mad, beat the dog, then threw him into the creek. The officer's found the dog's collar on the back steps."

Most of the crowd couldn't believe their ears, especially Margo and Kent. "Yep." The chief continued. "This guy is going away for a long time."

"At least they got him." The vet tech replied. The group individually spewed their own views about the owner and the situation. There weren't too many positive things said about the owner, go figure.

Vicki Ponson had spoken to the police when they arrived and then went over to he neighbors. Ten minutes later she had seen them lead him down the driveway in handcuffs and put into the back of the police car. She had also seen the dog rescued on tv and reports that he was doing well despite his terrible ordeal. This had given Vicki a feeling of pride in doing the right thing. Margo and Kent shared a similar feeling. They alerted the authorities and initiated the rescue call. They were there for all three attempts and knew full well that since this was no accident that the dog, Chocolate, would need a home. After a brief conversation with the vet tech and some information exchanged, once Chocolate makes a full recovery the vet hospital they would be in touch with his potentially new would-be owners, Margo and Kent.

"Thank you for all of your help." Margo directed her praise to all of the men and women who helped. The vet tech responded. "He needs recovery so it may be a while until he gets to go to his new home."

Margo looked up at Kent and smiled. "We will wait for him."

Family Memories

Posing With the Latest Catch

Growing up in an all Italian hunting and fishing family holds a special place in one's heart, and in one's photo album. The hunters of the Rizzo family consisted of my father, grandfather, uncles, and several cousins.

During each deer or turkey season the proud hunter would pose with his latest take from that season, bucks, does, turkeys, you name it. The pictures of the hunter and the prey almost always consisted of the same canine posing next to the newest trophy. She was a female beagle mix named Samantha. She was our family's first dog. Being part beagle and part collie, she sported a black, brown, tan, and white mixed coat of medium length. Samantha herself was not fond of hunting, but she loved to pose in the pics no matter if it was fall, winter, spring, or summer – she was in them all.

Our family had adopted Samantha in summer of 1992. It was mid July and the temperatures soared in the lower hundreds that day with the record-breaking heat and high humidity. Stepping out of the safety zone of air conditioning in the house or car was unbearable for more than a few minutes. Of course, this was the day we brought home our new dog.

All of us were excited, my parents had a Siamese cat previously for eighteen years, but I was fourteen and my brother was ten at the time and we wanted a dog. As it turned out my brother wasn't much of an animal person, and my mother was allergic to dogs, but that didn't stop us one bit. All of us rustled over the idea of which type of dog to get. We basically had the pick of the selection at the Erie Humane Society, because pure bred dogs from breeders were far too expensive. They had a beagle mix among their choices and since my father owned a beagle when he was growing up that was the same breed we chose. Sam was a young six months old when we brought her home and her playful demeanor was exactly what all of us needed.

My father did not teach Sam to be a hunting dog; she just didn't seem to have that instinct in her. She did love camping and the outdoors, but found it to be more preferable to lie under a shady tree versus running through the woods. The closest she had ever gotten to be a hunting dog was catching the occasional rabbit that tried to sneak under the back deck. So instead Sam posed with the hunting trophies and the hunters themselves. Each hunter needs that "hunting buddy" per se and in this case my father had an after-the-fact hunting buddy.

My family had several cabins in the mountains of north central Pennsylvania where all the entire family went hunting and camping. The clean fresh mountain air was relaxing to say the least and nothing was more fun than sitting under the dark starry nights with family by the fire pit. It was the perfect place to rest our feet and paws next to.

Being a grown woman now with my own family we also go camping at the same cabins a few times each year. My husband is an avid fisherman and hunter. Our youngest pup is his "hunting buddy in training" we like to call him. Tazz has taken quite well to the bird dog sport and is a wannabe fisherman himself. Tazz loves the water and his nickname is "The Water Pirate". All he needs is an eye patch and a good strong "Arrggg!" and that's all he needs to complete his title. Jason believes him to be half-fish; it must be the Labrador in him. With all of Tazz's natural instincts we expect that he will be found in quite a few photos in our family album - Posing with the latest catch.

Veronica and Peaches

Like any other teenage girl growing up I had a BFF, Veronica. We were two peas in a pod, as that expression goes. We were very much alike and also very much different. Veronica and I were the same age, only separated by a few months. Like everything else we had in common we were both dog people. I had Samantha and she had Peaches.

Though Veronica and I shared a lot of the same interests and did almost everything together we were also competitive sometimes. The same summer that I got Samantha she had also gotten Peaches. Peaches was an apricot poodle. Both dogs were the same age, just like us. Our taste in canine breeds went perfectly with our individual personalities. I preferred the down to Earth mixed-dog which tended to be light-hearted and Veronica had her pure-bred poodle, which at times seemed to be picky and high-strung.

She and I first became friends in middle school, half way through our sixth grade year. We were in most of the same classes and only occasionally talked. One day upon talking we came to find out, almost in disbelief, that we were related. My paternal grandmother was first cousins with her maternal grandmother. That made us third cousins. It was two generations later and we each had no clue until then that we were related.

Veronica and I both had a strong Italian heritage that we were extremely proud of and wore on our sleeves. There were family reunions, picnics, and occasions of all sorts that we both attended. Her grandmother, Nana, and her husband along with their family always celebrated Saint Joseph's Day. I was always invited, which meant a lot to me. In return I always invited Veronica to the Russo Family Reunion, being mostly Italians, which she had attended them as well. We had so much in common: work, boyfriends, shopping, friends, our heritage, and our dogs.

Like our similarities we also had our differences. We went to the same schools, but our home life and upbringings were different. I attended computer school at vo-tech and she was in the school chorus and plays. After high school we attended different colleges in the region. She stayed local, lived at home and went to a private catholic college while I stayed in a dorm at the local state university about twenty miles of town.

Little by little we separated due to time and space. We each had different goals, new friends, and we were busy living our lives. We occasionally saw each other during our college years here and there, but as fast as we became friends we also seemed to part just as sudden.

While I was in my dorm I had gotten a call from Veronica that her grandmother had passed away from a massive heart attack. She was upset and distraught, as anyone would be. I offered my condolences and felt just awful for her. The funeral was in the middle of the week and with me living out of town and no car of my own I was not able to attend the funeral. I believe that contributed to our drifting apart, with the passing of Nana. We were talking less and less and living our different lives. Once I had my daughter our friendship seemed almost non-existent and finally we lost touch.

Veronica and I were best friends for eight years and now is mostly a sweet memory of my past. Now with us being former friends I have not seen her in almost ten years.

Between the loss of relatives, and the distance of time

and distance we became friends as quickly as a picture placed on a mantle and lost of friendship just as quickly.

We had shared so much growing up. I was out of my parents' house when Samantha passed on and I did not have Veronica to share that moment with. She did not get to share the moment with me when Peaches passed on as well.

Despite our individual differences we also shared incredible likenesses. A BFF is someone to be valued and treasured. What remains now are the memories and cherished photos placed in a tightly-bound album. My favorite pic of Veronica was her senior class picture with her holding Peaches. I know how much Samantha meant to me as Peaches did to Veronica.

Melamine Pet Food Crisis – Part One

For so many American's the Melamine Pet Food Crisis of 2007 had hit too close to home. Many unfortunate cats and dogs had adversely experienced mild sickness with vomiting to death. The FDA recalled more than 100 brands of cat and dog food in 2007 from the discovery of Melamine in Wheat Gluten that was used in the pet food products.

"Melamine can be used to create products such as plastics, cleaning products, glues, inks, and fertilizers. Melamine has no approved use as an ingredient in human or animal food in the United States." FDA Release - February 6, 2008

In March 2007 the FDA was alerted by a manufacturer when fourteen cats had died in a taste test trial. From November 2006 to February 2007, three and a half month's time, over 800 tons of the purported wheat gluten was imported into the United States from China to be used in pet foods.

The tainted food had unfortunately affected Samantha, my parent's beagle and collie mix. Samantha, like so many other pets at the time had experienced vomiting and lethargy due to unknown reasons, she was sick and no one knew why. My father had left work early to come home and to find Samantha lying on her side on the kitchen floor having labored breathing. He called the nearby vet hospital and took her in immediately. The vet staff had seen a few cases of the same type of symptoms, all recently. This had happened prior to the warnings and pet food recalls.

Samantha was in kidney failure. Her brand of food was one of the brands that later on would be recalled. Samantha stayed at the animal hospital for a few days and was given various medications to help, but in the end there was nothing that could have been done. The only fortunate factor in Samantha's case was her age; she was twelve and had lived a full life. She was in an incredible amount of pain; regretfully and sadly Samantha had to be put to sleep. The pain meds had helped, but there was no possible action that could be taken to reverse the damage that was done to her kidneys.

Both of my parents were in attendance when Samantha was put to sleep. Her body was cremated and now sits in an urn on their mantel. Soon after Samantha's passing the pet food recalls and warnings were issued by the FDA. The media was in a frenzy with reports, articles, and accusations. Several FDA press releases were issued including one that found Melamine in a second pet food ingredient, being that of a rice protein.

Upon contacting the veterinarian who provided Samantha's care he, as well as my parents, had suspected that the Melamine caused the kidney failure. Since the cremation had already taken place there was no proof at this point, only the tests that were previously done. My parents were just as upset and angry as any other person in the country who was going through the exact same experience with their cat or dog. They had lost a member of the family for unneeded reasons.

The year following there were two separate indictments with a total of fifty-three counts and charges filed. The first Grand Jury case involved a Chinese firm, Xuzhou Anying Biologic Technology Development Co., LTD. (XAC), and a Chinese nationalist who exported plant proteins to the United States had twenty-six counts. The other twenty-seven counts were filed against ChemNutra, a Las Vegas, NV company, and ChemNutra's two owners for purchasing the exports from the Chinese company.

Two years after Samantha passed was when my parent's decided to get another dog. They wanted another beagle mix and had gone to the same Humane Society that they got Samantha from to look for one. That's when Maxwell was adopted and became a part of the family. With everything that happened to Samantha my father was more cautious about the type of dog food that they would feed Maxwell. He chose a brand that was not recalled. He wanted to be as cautious as possible and had put a lot of time and energy into researching dog food.

Maxwell's veterinarian and animal hospital is the same as Samantha's. My father has known the senior vet on staff there for twenty years and feels confident with their staff and the care they provide. Since the crisis the FDA has put strict regulations on all pet foods, requiring that they meet certain standards to unsure that quality and safe ingredients are used.

Picnicking Pets

"B-7!" was yelled out into the group and most had returned with an "Aww…" or a "No!" They were five minutes into the single bingo game with no takers.

"O-75!" Was bellowed in succession from the portly man with the stogie hanging from his lip. The crowd was littered with booing when one of my aunts yelled "Bingo!" She wins every year and no one seems to forget it. Shouts from the other side of the pavilion traveled to our side. "You Rizzo's can't win them all." It was true though, we did win most of them.

The Russo Family Reunion happens every year the first Sunday in July. They reserve the same pavilion every year in the same park. It's the largest of all the pavilions, having the best facilities. Though the shelter is a large one it still can barely hold all of the Italians whom fill it up, almost as many as a Yankee's game. There's young ones, older ones, and the four-legged ones. They come from all over the region and are all related.

The Russo's go back for many generations. To me it's my paternal grandmother's grandparents, if you can remember that. I sometimes can't. All I know is that I'm half Italian and half a mix of everything else. We all wear our green, white, and red proudly. In these uncertain times of being an American it's nice to have a heritage, a nationality to where you have a sense of history and pride that you cannot always get it from your residing country.

The reunion is a grand event. The above mentioned bingo game happens after lunch, but before the Chinese auction. It's ordered chaos at its best. This year the reunion fell on the same day as the Fourth of July; fireworks added to the festivities. One of my far-distant drunk relatives will be shooting off some illegal PA grade firework and probably set a tree on fire, memories are priceless.

A lot of people usually bring their pets, mostly dogs. Large ones, small ones, you name it. All are welcomed and all are adopted Italians. One year, however, someone brought a cat. That was a huge mistake.

These dogs eat like kings, especially at the picnic. While most dogs at most picnics are scrounging the ground these dogs have a buffet. Why beg for a modest piece of a crumb when you can have ox roast sandwich au jus, meatballs with sauce, and pasta salad. These dogs have it made.

My parents bring Maxwell as they had always used to bring Samantha. Maxwell more often than not was a welcomed addition to the Rizzo side of the pavilion. He'd get lots of attention from aunts, uncles, and cousins; he reveled in it. Stories and laughter about the good old days filled the air and "Italian Hour" would play on the radio. It was mostly instrumental versions of Frank Sinatra songs along with other classics.

This year Maxwell was top dog, most of my immediate family left their dogs at home. Max was in his moment. He had attention, food, and these people all to him until my cousin had came with one of their dogs. Rocco, the well-trained pit-bull mix was all black and looked like a gargoyle. He was sweet and obedient and didn't even need a leash. This however, was not acceptable to Max. It was go time. Max barked and pulled and acted like Rocky Balboa with his come-here-and-you'll-regret-it attitude.

My father was irritated with the two dogs. Rocco wanted to play and Max wanted to attack. "If I would have known they were bringing their dog I would have left Max at home." It's a typical saying and happens every year. To Max's benefit they only stayed for an hour or so since they had other picnics to attend. Max also felt relieved and he was back in charge with no opponents to challenge him.

Mid afternoon was the kids games; Amber took part and had fun tossing water balloons. Next year there should be doggy games. I'd organize and run it. It would be fun. Make up cute little treat bags for the picnicking pooches. Why not? Why should the two-leggers get to have all of the fun?

What can I say about families? Big or small they are yours; you belong to a group and have unity. Not like the groups found on Facebook or MySpace, but a real-life familiar and long-lasting group. There is no need to find acceptance online when you have it at home or in your own backyard. It is there, possibly at a reunion, all the people with

whom you share a special relation to are your relatives, friends, and pets. A simple occasion can reunite all with shared moments and memories over your favorite dish or possibly a fallen piece of food.

Personality & Mixed Breeds

Training

Dog training in itself is a science, a well-refined process of information and commands passed from human to canine. In most cases it is just as arduous for the trainer to learn and he or she needs to be more disciplined as the dog. Canines are intelligent animals with similar biology and thought processes to humans. Modern day dog training is more than a set of commands that the canines are supposed to follow. It was influenced from human psychology being applied to canines for behavioral benefits and was then further researched, used, and focused in dog training.

Rocky's obedience class was very structured and it worked as it should with time, effort, and discipline. Though throughout the whole experience I learned the process and the execution of the commands, but through my lack of education, knowledge, and naiveness I failed to see the intrinsic value of the origin of dog training and how scientists over the last three centuries influenced behavioral science and how it is applied to both humans and canines.

Through various life experiences I have developed a deeper respect for the process of dog training as learning is continuous. In addition to the formal education of high school and college so is learning for dogs beyond that of obedience class. The brain is just as any other muscle in the respect that it always needs to be worked and challenged, this is true for humans and their four-legged companions. I have vowed that Tazz's learning will continue through his life and not fall by the wayside.

Dog training has existed before, during, and after the applied science of operant conditioning. "Good trainers understand the whole dog." Breeds, genetics, individual characteristics, and environment effects how dogs learn, behave, and are trained. Canines are just as individual as the people who own them.

Genetics affects the canines in various ways. One element in particular is the color of the dog. Color has been thought to affect a dog's temperament and correlates to how and the degree of a dog's training. Their color heritage comes from their ancestors and often in the breed standard colors. Individualism, in respect to color, can determine in part whether the canine is more likely to be obedient or defiant. For example, in Poodles the standard color is black and any other variation predisposes the canine to more defiance in regards to training and obedience. The opposite it found in Labradors where as yellow is the more submissive color and black is more defiant. More often than not most service dogs for disabled people are the lighter colored labs rather than the darker colored labs for this reason.

So many other factors play a large role in the dog's individualism. A dog's natural disposition in regards to breed in a key element, but so is the dog's master and people's disposition whom surround the dog and compose the environmental factor. Though training itself will not change a dog's natural temperament the dog's disposition may change. If the master is orderly and demanding he or she more than likely will end up having an orderly and demanding dog. As where nervous and energetic persons have restless and overactive canines while laziness leads to laziness and so forth. Dogs and people alike pick up the non-verbal language of the humans and other animals in their environment and react. Typically dogs learn to mimic behaviors since they are the pack followers and the humans are the leaders of their pack.

With dispositions in mind and the fact that a person cannot change a dog's natural temperament through training a shy dog in nature will not change and become a strong-willed canine and therefore would not be a good watchdog. The hardest canine's to train, in regards to their disposition, is the suspicious canines. This is one reason why wild and domestic cross-breeds are not reliable or trainable. The suspicious canine does not want to learn to follow. If a canine is not submissive to the human and not willing to take its natural place in the family pack then training the canine will not change it as it will not conform well to domestic life. Other common problems with dog's disposition are canine's that are shy, lazy, silly, and clowny.

The most influential behavioral scientists from the 1800's until today were Ivan Pavlov (1849 – 1936), Edward Lee Thorndike (1874 – 1949), J.B. Watson (1878 – 1958), and B.F. Skinner (1904 – 1990). Through the pioneering studies of these scientists behavioral operant condition was studied, tested, and widely used throughout the world. Human analysis had spread to the canine application as well.

The most important two factors to operant conditioning are the use of primary and secondary reinforcers. The primary reinforcer is used upon the successful completion of a task or behavior and typically food is used as the primary reinforcer. After the dog masters the task / behavior with the primary reinforcer a secondary

reinforcer is usually used in concurrence. This would be using praise such as "Good Boy!" Both of these are used in basic obedience training. "Reinforcement occurs when a behavior, followed by a consequent stimulus, is strengthened, or becomes more likely to occur again." The use of positive reinforcers with consistent training is imperative for the successful training of the dog.

In the process of training Tazz, his willingness to learn has been unsurpassed. Since he is half German Shepherd he loves to work and also being half Labrador he is eager to learn and please. For most dogs *sit* is the first command and the easiest to master. Next, for Tazz, came *shake.* Where after he sits he lifts either paw as to "shake" someone's hand. In addition to the basics we have been working on his retrieving skills as he is eager to be Jason's hunting buddy. He loves playing fetch and retrieving a tennis ball like most other dogs. However, we add a series of specific vocal commands and hand signals that Tazz has been able to learn quickly.

A typical game of fetch sounds like the following:

"Tazz *get!*" a tennis ball is thrown. Tazz gets the ball and returns with it. With the command "Tazz *give.*" and a hand gesture of a cupped hand Tazz knows to drop the ball when he reaches our feet. The combination of specific one-word commands and a hand signal for each along with the dog's name gives the dog a clear-cut command that he knows it is time to work and listen. I have had all positive experiences using this type of method when doing basic and ancillary dog training.

Puppies are socialized and learn through either play or serious training. Play occurs from the time they are with their litter mates and onward. It is the socialization that helps give the dogs their foundation. Puppies and dogs learn from other puppies and dogs just as children learn from their parents. Each dog has a vocabulary; a lot of dogs recognize *toy* and *ride*, but for Tazz his two favorite words are *hunting* and *gunshot*. However, Baby Girl's favorite word is *Baby Girl*, she knows that she is the topic of the conversation.

Since I have more experience with dog training it has been a challenge for Jason to train Tazz. Yes, trainers need trained. He has never "formally" trained any of his previous dogs and if Tazz is to be his hunting dog then he needs to learn the training process. Tazz knows and has chosen Jason to be his master. Jason has the most natural authority with Tazz and Tazz is most willing to listen to him. In fact, even at the young age of three months Tazz does not require a leash to stay with Jason, he just goes obediently with him. I have always considered myself to be a "dog person" until I met Jason. Almost every dog he seems meet loves him.

I am mostly responsible for Baby Girl's training. We had gotten Baby Girl prior to getting Tazz and over time she had learned the basic commands. Baby Girl had come a long way with heeling and walking versus running and sprinting everywhere, but that in part that is the Siberian Husky's nature, to run and sprint.

Science has given humans the insight to see why dogs are the way they are in everything through their thought processes, physical make-up, appearances, temperament, and all their god-given natural abilities. Even the most experienced and savvy dog trainer cannot repress nature and the canine's heredity instincts. If all dogs were exact copies of the cookie-cutter standard then there would be no variety and no individuality. Personally, when it comes to training, I prefer a challenge.

Shelter Dogs

I've known some pretty good shelter dogs in my time, and I even adopted a few of them. In addition to breeders there are animal shelters, such as a Humane Society, or rescue groups. Both are excellent places to find, see, and meet a potential adoptee. There are canines all over the country who need to be placed in good homes at any given point in time.

You can find a variety of dog breeds at shelters. Occasionally you may find a pure bred dog, but more often than not there are a large variety of mix breeds. In my opinion, mixes have the best of both breeds and there is nothing wrong with a little variety. A lot of wonderful canines come out of animal shelters and are happily adopted into good homes. Rocky and Maxwell are perfect examples, along with all of the other dogs throughout the country.

In addition to visiting your local Humane Society there is another valuable tool in which you can locate almost any shelter pet in the country, www.petfinder.com. With this website you can do a broad or advanced search into canines or felines along with location, breed, size, age, and general temperament. These are just a few of the search criteria available on the site. I have found it to be a useful tool in locating specific types of dogs.

Visiting a shelter is the best way to see these animals first hand. Dogs are just as individual as people are. Some are shy, some are outstanding, most want to play, but all want to be loved. There are a wide range of reasons why these dogs are available for adoption. Some dogs are there due to moving, divorce, change in work or lifestyle, or financial reasons. Whatever the reason these dogs have been carefully evaluated during the intake process and over a set amount of time the staff determines what type of individual or family would best match the pet.

The staff tests the dog's compatibility and looks for traits, strengths, and weaknesses in several areas. How does the dog get along with other dogs? children? cats? How is the dog's temperament? Is there food aggression? Is the dog shy? How does the dog play? These are only a few of the questions that the staff deduces from the evaluation and answers those questions in order to make the best canine-human match. In addition to behavioral aspects of the dog the dog is also checked and tested for its health and physical condition. Is the dog spayed / neutered? Any parasites present? Any physical conditions exist that potential owners need to be aware of? Does the canine have any special needs? The dog is checked through veterinarian exams by both licensed vets and vet students. After these processes have been completed each animal now has a *pet profile*.

The pet profiles are the single sheet of laminated paper that hangs from the canine's kennel and is also loaded into the pet finder's website for search and informational purposes.

I have met some awesome shelter dogs who have found great homes. A few to mention are Big Brad (purebred German Shepherd), Diablo (Black Lab and Doberman Pincher mix), and Diesel (Golden Retriever and Yellow Lab mix). These were just a few large breed dogs that Jason and I were considering for adoption. In the end, we ended up going with the Siberian Husky puppy, Baby Girl.

Some other great adopted shelter dogs were my dog Rocky (Black Lab and Rottweiler mix) and my parent's dog Maxwell (Beagle and Bassett Hound mix). Some adoption choices are easy, like Rocky was for me. He was a four month old puppy at the time whose original name was Blackie. For some people the choice is harder such as the choice my parents made with Maxwell. He was six months old and was in the same kennel as his brother, Charlie. Charlie had more of a Beagle look to him and originally my parents favored him more. They considered adopting both, but in the end had decided on only adopting Maxwell. Maxwell barked less and was less destructive than Charlie.

Humane Societies consist of paid staff and volunteers. These organizations are supreme advocates for canines and the fair treatment of them. The NWPA Humane Society often hosts awareness days with activities for children. Amber and I have attended several of these where there are children's story telling, crafts, snacks, and a chance to meet the dogs. We often enjoy going to various shelters to see the dogs and the facilities.

Organizations like these do receive grants and some funding, but more than that rely strongly on donations and pet adoption fees. Shelters, along with the staff and volunteers, provide a much needed service to communities of providing temporary homes to animals until a permanent home can be found and every pet should have a home.

I'll Have My Breeds??? Mixed!

While purebred canines have a pureness and undeniable value to them in regards to their genetics it cannot be denied that some mixed breeds are also nearly perfect. The canine with two or more well chosen breeds can have a conglomerate blending of traits to provide the best of both characteristics. We have seen this in several newer mixes such as the Labradoodle.

There are lesser known mixes such as the Germador, and a sometimes-combination of Bull Dog and Shih Tzu. On a recent fine Memorial Day weekend I had the pleasure of meeting my parent's new neighbors, Darius, Brenda, their son Mack, and their four-year old dog Chloe. Chloe is an adorable pooch consisting of Bichon Frise' and Poodle breeds. I questioned myself asking "Would this mix be a

Bichondle? Or perhaps a Poodlise'?" I myself am still not sure. Of course it would not be recognized by the AKC, but in turn the canine's personality needs to fit well with the family, and that is the most important thing.

Not only do most canine groups not recognize mixed breeds, neither does the state of Pennsylvania. I had found this out first hand by applying for and obtaining a dog license for both of my dogs. The New Year brought snow, icy roads, and dog tags so I stopped into the closest Agway, which advertised dog license sales. It was eight dollars for both my dogs, since neither was fixed at the time. Upon completing the application forms for each canine the box for 'breed' read as 'Siberian Husky' for Baby Girl and 'Labrador Retriever and German Sherpard' for Tazz. However, when the employee entered the information and printed out the form under breed it correctly listed 'Siberian Husky', but Tazz's form read 'Mixed'.

"What?" I questioned the employee who replied that the state doesn't recognize individual breeds of the canine if the canine is of mixed breeds.

The Marcsons acquired Chloe when she was eight weeks old. Darius, being a rather large man wanted to get a dog for this wife, yet when the tiny pup was placed in his large palm that was it. The dog was now his and he pampers his pooch to the extreme. Another question I often ask myself. *I wonder how often a spouse or parent gets a dog for another member of the family, but the intended ownership is relinquished?* This was the case with Darius and Chloe.

"What breed of dog is she?" asked Jason.

"She's Bichon Frise' and Poodle." Darius replies. The topic of interest of our conversation was solely on Chloe now.

In careful observation of the dog there are characteristics of both breeds that are expressive. She is pure white and physically resembles the Bichon except for the legs, which are a tad longer and skinnier, and also the nose and tongue are more elongated like poodles. Both breeds are of the non-sporting category, are from French descent, and are also known as companion dogs. In my opinion these two breeds as a mix complement each other nicely both in physical appearance and temperament. Of course, the Marcsons feel the same about their perfect pooch and loyal friend, Chloe.

The combination of mixed breeds are endless, you can have a Dalmadane for the large breed lover or a Yorkshire Tzu for the tiny toy lovers. A good hunting dog could be a Curly-coat Spaniel and an excellent working and winter-weather dog may be the Alaskan Husky. The possibilities are endless and though most organizations want owners to spay and neuter their dogs and discourage inter-mixing of different breeds. The problem with this frame of mind is that you just never know if the best possible watchdog for your property, for example, could be a Doberman Mastiff.

Throughout the history of the domesticated canine, which evolved and were derived from the wild canine, humans had observed and bred different canines for specific reasons. Working dogs, water dogs, herding dogs, gun dogs, and small rodent elimination dogs are only to name a few. The domesticated canines had tasks and jobs to perform based on their abilities, but with the passing of time people rely less and less on their four-legged workers. Though a lot of dogs still have and perform jobs, i.e. search and rescue or therapy dogs are just a few to mention, the majority of canines had stayed at man's side and have taken on the roll of 'pet'.

One of the newest canine trainings in cancer-sniffing dogs; it is performance with a purpose. These dogs are extensively trained and vigorously tested for accuracy. It is a job that no human can perform. With the ever changing world we need to change to keep up with it and so do our canine companions. A mingling of different breeds to produce a canine that can perform certain tasks that humans are not able to do. In turn, these dogs should be encouraged and commended.

Dogs are meant to naturally perform at man's side. First and foremost dogs should be treated humanely and with the utmost respect, and should also have a job. Each dog should have a task – large or small – every pet contributes to a person or persons. Whether it's putting a smile on an elderly couple's face or pulls a child out of a frozen snow bank each one is invaluable and needs to be treated as so.

So in the case of the Marcson's canine. Weighing in the personality traits, physical characteristics, mannerisms I have concluded that Chloe is not necessarily a Bichondle or a Poodlise', but instead is just Chloe. The sweet white-colored mix is proudly herself day in and day out and is contented with being a wonderful pet.

To each their own as the saying goes.

Negatives on Health Issues

Lyme Happens

Lyme disease is an all too common problem in certain areas of the United States. New York, Massachusetts, Connecticut, and Pennsylvania are among the top states for reported cases of Lyme disease in humans and canines. It is mostly spread by deer ticks. These millimeter-sized terrorists hang about in trees and bushes and look for a host to attach themselves to. They sense animals and people from the heat of their bodies and go towards the unsuspecting victim, once attached they live off of and suck blood from the host. If not removed immediately the Lyme can be transmitted to the host. If you are alive then you are a heat source and could be a potential target and at risk to be bitten by a tick and contracting Lyme disease, among other diseases.

Being an avid outdoors person I have been lucky to only have been bitten by a tick once. I found it and removed it immediately. The bite mark was clearly visible and a red area surrounding the bite site was already beginning to swell. Immediately I was worried and did some extra research on ticks and Lyme. I knew the chance of contracting Lyme was very small, but still worried I went to the emergency room. The ER doctor diagnosed it as a tick bite, which I knew, but I was concerned about getting an antibiotic. I felt more relieved once I had the Penicillin in my system and I did not worry as much about an infection.

On top of the antibiotic it was recommended to me to take an allergy medicine and after that all I could do is pay extra attention to the bite site for changes and watch for symptoms, which could appear within six weeks. After a week the red circular swelled area was gone and the bite injection area itself was almost healed. I was lucky, in any given year there are between two-thousand to five-thousand people who get Lyme disease in the state of Pennsylvania alone. On the other hand some states have had only five reported cases in the last five years, such as South Dakota. I would like to live in South Dakota rather than Pennsylvania when it comes to ticks.

The most serious case of Lyme disease that I have seen in a person was in one of my previous supervisors, Janine. Janine had found a tick attached in between her toes a few summers ago. Janine, her husband, son, and dog often spent their weekends in the next county south at a campground where they had a permanent site. She often wore sandals and disregarded "the pebble" which remained attached to her for a day or two. She noticed the tick and was horrified and had it removed. The same weekend her dog, a six-year old beagle named Jake, also had a tick found on him and it was removed right away.

Everything was fine and normal with Jake and Janine following the discovery of the tick. Jake continued to be fine, while Janine was not. Too much time had passed while the tick was attached and she had contracted Lyme disease. She was diagnosed with it while in ICU. Janine had a type of mini-stroke and experienced paralysis. She was immediately taken by ambulance to the hospital where she was admitted to ICU and was in a partial coma for nearly a week. The Lyme was discovered among the blood tests that were done at the hospital and Janine came close to death and coded twice. After rounds and rounds of IV antibiotics given she thankfully came out of the coma and some of the paralysis diminished. She was moved out of ICU, but still remained in the hospital for another week on a step-down unit. She continued to get better and was finally released.

Janine had undergone physical therapy for her face in the weeks and months after being discharged. Some of the Lyme continued to remain in her system and now only affects her face; it is still slightly drooping on the left side. The muscles in her left eye and her left law line still sometimes twitch. Janine has been thankful for her recovery even though some of the condition still persists. A few facial ticks here and there and is most certainly better than death, which luckily did not occur.

Janine still goes to their campground with her family, but is leery now of wearing sandals and is more cautious, and of course has plenty of bug and tick repellent. Jake is still tick-free thanks to a variety of dog tick repellents and Lyme vaccinations.

Previous to Janine's experience yet another family friend and her pets have negatively been affected by Lyme disease. Several hundred miles from where Janine lives is where my family's cabin is located. It's just east of the Allegheny National Forest, west of the Pennsylvania Grand Canyon, and right in the middle of deer tick country. The cabin is in a hollow tucked on the side of a mountain in north central PA, *Knotty-Pine-Hide-Away* we named it. It's a picturesquely-forested area and is reluctantly infested with deer ticks.

Butch and Dorothy are the retired couple who permanently reside next to my family's cabin. Dorothy has on

71

a few occasions been tested positive for Lyme. Dorothy's outcome from the Lyme was luckily not as serious as Janine's, but she still had been inflicted. Dorothy has had some slight paralysis on her right arm, and had undergone the same type of antibiotic treatment and physical therapy. Sadie III, a two-year old Shih Tzu, luckily has not contracted Lyme and Butch and Dorothy have taken all the necessary precautions to try to prevent ticks getting on her, and themselves as well.

Besides Dorothy's affliction with Lyme, Sadie III was preceded by Sadie I and Sadie II, all were Shih Tzu's and all were female. The first two Sadie's were bitten by deer ticks and they had contracted Lyme disease, and regretfully died. It has been heart-breaking for Butch and Dorothy to go through several dogs in several years. They never took the Shih Tzu's in the woods and they were confined to only their yard, but despite their efforts the ticks still got on people and pets, as in this case. The loss of her first two dogs due to Lyme has been difficult for both of them; especially Dorothy who herself has Lyme and still relies on a cane for support of her right side.

Sadie III should be a tick prevention advocate and thus far has been fortunate. In addition to putting spray repellent on humans and drops on dogs there should be more that can be done to keep ticks out of yards. There needs to be a mass market for Deet candles being similar to what citronella candles do to repel mosquitoes. Lyme disease is responsible for numerous deaths per year and extra measures need to be taken for prevention. These are needless illnesses and deaths, in both humans and canines, which occur and should not happen.

Devastating Rabies

Thomas's family went to the Humane Society to look for a dog. Thomas was ten and his sister Bethany just turned eight. Their parents had thought that Thomas and Bethany were at a good age to get a dog. The responsibility would be good for them. Thomas's mother had several small dogs growing up and Thomas's father only had one dog. Even until now his father was leery of dogs, but he wanted what was best for this two children.

The Humane Society was recently remodeled and was beautiful inside. They had all types of puppies, dogs, cats, and kittens, plus a few long-floppy-eared bunnies. Thomas admired German Shepherds the most because they had reminded him of police dogs. There were two at the Humane Society. Upon speaking with the children the only breed of dog that Thomas father did not want was a German Shepherd. Thomas asked and begged for one for months from his father. Thomas knew his father had one when he was a boy and figured that he would want another one. A few days before going to the Humane Society Thomas's father told him the devastating truth of what happened to Buzz, his German Shepherd.

The year was 1975 and Thomas's father Charles, Charlie, at the time was eleven years old. He had a three year old German Shepherd, Buzz. The pair was inseparable. Charlie was the pitcher and some times played short-stop for their youth baseball team, The Beavers.

Veterinarian care, like any other medical field, was not then what it is today. Charlie's parents did not have much money for proper vet care and shots, yet Buzz was in great health despite the lack of veterinarian care.

The family had lived in a small community just on the outskirts of a large city. Eventually the area would be turned into a subdivision. The southern side of Cranberry, opposite of the city, was flanked by a large wooded area. The small ball field which was the home field to The Beavers and also the high school was tucked in next to the woods.

One baseball game, on a particular Friday night, Charlie played ball as he often did. At this game his older sister Dana, his parents, and Buzz were all in attendance. Charlie was the star pitcher for the beginning of the game and finished up playing the short stop position. Dana was in charge of Buzz that night. She was older, being sixteen, and wanted to hang out with her friends instead of watching Charlie's dog and being at the game. She sat near the front left corner of the stands so she could tie Buzz's leash to the railing. Charlie's parents sat by the neighbors and were up a few rows on the stands.

The Beavers were defeating the Black Jays by a score of six to five and it was near the bottom of the eighth inning. Dana had seen her best friend show up with a few boys from her school. Dana had figured Buzz to be fine since the leash was tied and she took off to meet up with her friends. Charlie's parents were deep into a conversation about politics and what Jimmy Carter was doing for the country and paid no attention to Dana or Buzz.

Buzz did not like being left alone and saw Charlie up at bat and barked a few times. He pulled and tugged his leash against the railing and the knot was slowly slipping. He had noticed a small flock of crows near the woods just past the ball field. Buzz pulled and pulled. Finally the knot gave out; Buzz was free and off running towards the crows. Dana was nowhere to be found and Charlie's parents didn't notice that Buzz was free right away until the gasps and the crowd concerns had alerted them. His father went after Buzz. Charlie saw Buzz running, but now he was on second base as he had hit the ball on the first swing.

The game was over within the next few minutes and The Beavers won by an eight to five finishing score. Charlie did not waste time with congratulations from his teammates. He was off towards the woods towards where Buzz had been running. Dana had heard the news and both her and her mother headed down to the woods as well.

"I trusted you!" Charlie had run up to his sister yelled at her.

"It's not my fault. I had him tied." Dana snottily replied and did not show much concern for Buzz or her brother. Charlie's father had walked out of the woods with a few others. He walked over to his son and put his hand on Charlie's shoulder.

"I couldn't find him. It's almost dark. We need to go, but can come back in the morning. Don't worry. Your sister will be punished." Charlie had protested; he wanted to find Buzz. His father's words were of no comfort to him.

Charlie stayed up most of the night as tomorrow was Saturday and there was no school. He made nearly a dozen *lost dog* flyers and planned to put them up around his neighborhood and the nearby blocks as soon as the sun came up. Charlie had asked his father if he could write on the flyers about a reward, but his father had sadly said no. They didn't have much money as it was and could not afford to pay a reward. This had upset Charlie, but in the end motivated him even more to find his dog. Charlie was out of the house at seven in the morning. The sun was up for nearly an hour, but his mother did not want him going out earlier than that.

First Charlie put up a few fliers then he went back home to pack a few supplies to take in the woods. He was going to look for Buzz and his father had agreed to accompany Charlie. If something was wrong with Buzz he would need a grown up and his father more than he ever had before. The two of them took the short drive to the ball field and the woods. It was only five minutes away, but his father wanted to get the car as close to the field as he could. Charlie put up most of the fliers around the ball field and down the street as well.

The weather was nice for walking, but to Charlie it might as well have been raining or snowing, He didn't care. He just wanted his dog back. They stayed on the trails and did not want to stray off too far and have them get lost in the woods as well. They walked for an hour or so Charlie had heard a faint whimpering coming from the right side towards the west. His father decided to leave some markers of paper as they walked so they could find their way back to the main trail. The woods were dense and in some spots the sunlight was unable to find its way down to the ground. All was calm and peaceful except for the whimpering that grew louder the further that they went.

Charlie and his father crossed a small run and continued. Charlie stopped suddenly and yelled "Buzz!" and sprinted towards him.

"Wait Charlie!" his father yelled. They both ran, but his father wanted to be cautious in case Buzz was hurt or something was wrong. His father came up to Buzz first. His leash was wrapped around a tree and it looked as if his front paw was bleeding. Buzz was licking it trying to clean the wound.

"Ok boy. It's ok." Charlie tried to reassure Buzz who was now trying to stand up and was wagging his tail wildly.

Charlie's father handed him the backpack and they unloaded a few first aid supplies and a canister of water. They were all excited, especially Charlie whose worries subsided and was beyond happy to find his dog. The father cleaned out Buzz's wound. He held his paw and said.

"It looks like some sort of bite on his paw." Charlie didn't seem to care, he untangled the leash while his father cleaned and wrapped the wound.

Buzz got up and limped. He panted and struggled with the pain as he tried to walk, but mostly hobbled with his owners back to the trail and out of the woods. They felt joy and were blessed and Charlie could not wait to get Buzz home. His father helped Buzz get into the backseat of their olive green and tan station wagon. They were on their way home. To Charlie and his father a family tragedy had been adverted.

That night Charlie took down all of the lost dog fliers and could not wait to go to the ballgame to tell all of his friends that Buzz was safe. Buzz had stayed home for the next few games. It gave Charlie a sense of security that he could not run off. Buzz healed just fine, though he was not taken to a vet. He was happy and all was normal for the next few weeks.

Nearly two weeks passed and Charlie had noticed that Buzz was not acting like himself. He was out in his dog house and did not want to come out when Charlie called him. Buzz walked around and circled, but did not come out. Charlie shrugged it off and went to get his dog food and water. He filled the water and noticed that Buzz was still inside circling like a shark would. Then Charlie began to pour the food out into his bowl. Just then Buzz seemed to snap. He darted out of the dog house and went directly for the food and inhaled it then dark the water just as fast. Charlie stood back and was bewildered. He'd never seen Buzz go after food or water like that. Charlie thought maybe he was sick and decided just to leave him. He thought he would be better in a day or two.

"It'll be ok boy." He said to Buzz as he lapped up the rest of the water in the bowl. Buzz let out a low growl and Charlie shrugged it off and went inside. The team had a few big games over the next couple of days. His sister had been sick and his mother was busy and concerned with her care while his father was working late most nights. Besides feeding Buzz Charlie had no time to play and he just hung around the yard and dog house alone.

A few more days had passed and now Buzz was becoming angrier and more rabid by the minute. He was changing and no one in the family had noticed until it was too late. Charlie's mom heard constant barking and growling coming from outside. She looked out the window and saw nothing. She figured Buzz had been inside the dog house. *What could he be barking at?* She wondered to herself. She often was busy and didn't take of Buzz much, but she ventured out into the backyard. It was two in the afternoon and the mailman had just passed and soon the kids would be home from school. Dana had gotten better and this was her first day back in almost a week. She saw that Buzz's bowl was empty and got some water to fill it. She filled the bowl with the pitcher of water and looked down and noticed that Buzz's leash had been chewed up and the pieces were lying on the ground. If Buzz was not feeling well she did not want to deal with it. She decided to go in the house and call her husband at work. He would deal with it when he got home.

She was about halfway back to the house and the growling started back up again. Charlie's mother standing there is her house dress and white apron with the pitcher in hand turned around and looked at the dog house. The sight was terrifying. Buzz was partly out of his dog house. His eyes were blaring and wild looking. His coat looked matted and chewed up as if he had been biting himself. She felt a surge of panic and ran for the house. Behind her she heard gravel flying and determined barking approaching her from behind. He dropped the pitcher, and ran up the three porch steps with efficiency. She opened the back door and closed it just in time. Buzz was at the door barking wildly and viciously. He was slamming his body against the back door trying to get in.

He was not able to break the glass window on the door so she was able to look at him through it. He was drooling uncontrollably with white foam pouring out.

"Oh my God! He has rabies!" She exclaimed in horror and went directly for the phone. First she called he husband. She was in tears while she dialed. Her husband's direct line at his desk just rang and rang. She was then transferred to a receptionist whom she instructed to have her husband call her immediately.

Buzz was still outside barking. She looked out the window to see him circling the porch. The next phone call she made was to the police. They were sending two cars over immediately along with animal control. She stayed in her kitchen looking at the wild animal that used to be their dog. She was thankful that none of the kids were home and so far no one was hurt. She called all of her neighbors and told them what happened and asked that they didn't go outside. Then she called her husband again. This time she got through.

"Didn't Patricia give you the message?!" She screamed over the phone and was panicking now. She had tried to keep her cool as long as she could, but now she sobbed and told him what happened.

"I'm on my way." He left the office in a hurry and wanted to get home as soon as he could.

Charlie's mother kept an eye on Buzz. She figured that if he tried to leave the yard she would open the door and try to keep his attention until the police got here. She thought of poor Charlie, how awful this would be on him. She then heard the grandfather clock chiming in the dining room. It was three o'clock and the kids were due home any minute.

Luckily the police arrived with animal control. There were three vehicles with four policemen and two animal control officers. All had weapons of some sort and she felt a little comfort, but not much. The yard was not fenced in and Buzz could run anywhere. *At least the kids aren't home yet.* She thought and was grateful for that fact. Buzz saw the officers coming towards him and he crouched down and growled loudly. Two officers and one animal control officer went down the driveway for a frontal approach and the other group went on the other side of the house in case the dog would run in that direction. All were prepared to take the dog down no matter what.

Buzz leapt up and lunged towards one of the officers. Back up was arriving as was Charlie's school bus had pulled up to the bus stop down the block. The kids got off the bus and Charlie saw the police cars down the street in front of his house and he went running. Charlie had no idea what was going on and the last thing that he thought of was Buzz. One officer fired, but missed. Buzz was furious with anger inside of him and he lunged a few more times. He was still foaming, barking, and out of control. Rabies was nothing to mess around with and the officers knew to take him down before anyone got hurt.

Buzz ran past the officers and around to the front of the neighbor's house. By now a crowd had grown and because of curiosity they felt the need to watch. After they saw the sight of the rabid dog most of them ran or sought protection somewhere. Police and fire trucks had one side of the street closed. An officer stopped Charlie and wouldn't let him pass. Charlie did not see Buzz right away, but he had the feeling that something bad was going to happen.

Charlie's father drove up soon after and he all he could do was watch. His wife was in the house terrified and he saw Charlie down at the end of the street with the police and firemen. Buzz was in front of his neighbor's house gleaming at what was left of the crowd. The officers steadied their aim again and were ready to fire their weapons at the rabid dog. Buzz looked at all the men scanning for his target. One of the police officers, who were closest to Buzz, looked slightly to the left and saw a man emerging from his house.

"Get back in!" The officer shouted.

The momentary distraction of the officer was all that Buzz needed and he went for his target. Buzz hurdled towards him with lightning speed. The officer shot but missed. It was too late. In the series of seconds Buzz had run, jumped, and taken a large chunk of the officer's arm off. Two of the other police officers fired at Buzz shooting him down. Charlie had dodged the street barricade and nearly made it to his house. From two doors down in a front lawn Charlie had seen what Buzz did to the officer and saw the officers kill Buzz in return.

Everyone at the scene breathed a sigh of relief when the animal was down except for Charlie and his parents. His mother saw Charlie and came rushing out of the house. She ran up to him and hugged him.

"Charlie thank God you are ok!" She exclaimed with tears streaming down her face. His face was similar. The animal control officers had the immediate area around the

81

dog blocked and were preparing to take the body and test it before disposal of it. Charlie was enraged and wanted to say goodbye to his dog. Due to quarantine issues it was not allowed to happen.

The police officer had to undergo several surgeries on his arm and was in the hospital for weeks and he also had to undergo physical therapy. Charlie's family did everything they could to help the officer and wanted to make it up to him and his family, but there was no possible way to do that. The police officer knew the risk of the job and despite what happened to him he was thankful that no one else had gotten hurt. The neighbors and community had different ideas, views, and feelings towards what happened. Most of the neighbors blamed Charlie's father for not providing the dog with the proper vet care and shots in the first place and the whole community tried to chastise him for not taking the dog to a veterinarian after they found it hurt in the woods. Other people had taken a neutral stance and decided the family and the injured office have been through enough.

Charlie had nightmares. He'd seen a child psychologist for the year following the incident and eventually the nightmares decreased. Their family did not get another dog after that. Charlie did not even want to be near dogs. When he was seventeen he dated his high school sweetheart and eventually married her. She had three small dogs; they were all Cavalier King Charles Spaniels. He felt comfortable in the fact that these dogs were much smaller than him. It took him a while to adjust, but he finally was able to.

Charlie and his wife had discussed getting a dog for Thomas and Bethany. Of course, German Shepherd's or any other large breed for that matter was out of the question. Charlie felt confident that if his children chose a small dog that he could control it if the unthinkable ever happened. Charlie's parents were glad to hear that their grandchildren were finally getting a dog, and that Charles was finally ready to move on.

They continued to walk around the Humane Society inventorying the canines. Thomas knew how his dad felt now about large dogs and understood why. He was happy to be there with them and his little sister looking at the small dogs. They finally made a selection and a Miniature Pinscher named Marsel was chosen. Thomas knew who he was and what he wanted to do when he got older. He wanted to be a police officer and have a German Shepherd K-9 Unit. He always admired them and the work that they did. This Pinscher was a good family dog for him, his sister, and especially his dad, but when he got older he was going to have his large dog, his large career, and with them the even larger responsibility.

Parasites Happen

In addition to Lyme disease and Rabies there are several types of internal, external, and bacteria diseases that affect canines and some can be contracted by humans. Whether your dog has a championship bloodline with pedigree or a mixture of breeds they are all susceptible to parasites. In the experiences that I have had with my own dogs there were two instances of parasite infections that unfortunately afflicted two of my puppies, one externally and one internally.

I came to find out that Rocky had an external parasite, Ringworm (*demodectic mange*). I found out at the oddest place, my daughter's pediatrician office. I had taken her in due to an odd rash on her hand. Upon the exam her doctor had informed me that it was Ringworm. Amber was two at the time and I had just gotten Rocky a few months before. The pediatrician asked if I had any pets and yes we had a new puppy. This turned out to be the culprit and was the source of the Ringworm. Amber was given a treatment of medicine and lotion which cleared up the rash.

Upon getting home I called the vet office to schedule an appointment and quarantined Rocky. I examined his fur and looked for any bald patches. There were two, one on each of his front legs. This was the infected site. Rocky was going in to the vet's that afternoon which comforted me somewhat, but first I had the task of cleaning and washing everything of Rocky's. I washed his pet bed and blankets, cleaned the floors and his toys, and replaced all of his chewies. The vet appointment that afternoon confirmed the Ringworm; he was given meds and lotions, same as Amber. Ringworm affects both canines and humans; when a person's skin touches the infected area, in the case of Ringworm, the infection is transmitted.

When I had first heard the word *parasite* a wave of panic shot through me and in most cases immediate proper veterinarian care treatment will remedy the infection. My second, and worst, situation dealing with parasites that I had seen occurred three days after we had gotten Tazz.

Jason and I could tell that Tazz was not feeling well from the first day we brought him home. His stomach was making unsettling noises and was upset most of the time. He seemed to have a fever by his dry and warm nose. It was the day after Christmas, a Saturday morning when he finally had gotten sick. I was grateful that Amber was staying at my parent's house for a week and she did not have to witness Tazz being physically sick. I was astonished and horrified when Tazz's bowel movement that morning was filled with large wiggly spaghetti-looking worms. I felt sick and Jason became sick. The sight was sickening and at least Tazz felt

better, too bad I couldn't say the same for us. Jason called his boss and described the worms and asked what we could do and I got online and did some researching.

It was Roundworm (*Toxocara*). Since the vet's office was not going to be open for two more days I found a liquid over-the-counter medication to give puppies and dogs for the treatment of Roundworm. After trekking through the snow and driving ten miles to our nearest Wal-Mart I found they had quite the selection and they were inexpensive. After returning, Tazz happily slobbered up the orange colored liquid and we he had given him a tiny piece of eggshell and yoke also. Between all that and his shot a few days later Tazz was all better, leaving parasites behind and he has been "parasite free" ever since.

Other common parasites found in canines, and humans can contract most of these as well, are hookworms, tapeworms, whipworms, heartworms, sarcoptic mange and others. Thankfully, I hope not to have anymore experiences with parasites.

Vaccines – One Size Fits All?

Just as parents exert proactiveness when it comes to their children's health, dog owners do the same for their canines. Of those dog owners, it's the dog lovers, whom at heart view their dogs as their children; they are loved, raised, and cared for.

The veterinarian and dog care system has many dynamics to its flow. There are veterinarians, organizations, boards, ethics and standards, staff, volunteers, groomers, kennelers, owners, families, and dogs, along with other components, all of which play an important role in the canine's health. The quality of care, more over, does not necessarily result from the quantity of money that one has. It doesn't buy happiness, or the best vet care for that matter, and the dogs certainly have no use for it.

In revisiting ethics, a very serious and often overlooked factor which plays a large role in a dog's vet care is in the vaccines. Often the damage is unknowingly done months before the vaccine reaches the vet office. It's produced by a pharmaceutical company, it's packaged, then shipped, and administered.

Every year millions of dogs are vaccinated and there are reported cases of side effects and unreported cases. In fact, several studies report that nearly only one percent of the adverse reactions and side effects are reported, per the WSAVA (World Small Animals Veterinarian Association). The reactions have been reported from a mild sickness to death. As with all medications and vaccines there are risks, but the highest percentage of all serious reactions comes from the administration of combination vaccines.

Small breeds are the most effected and susceptible to these reactions because of their weight. As researched the top breeds are: Dachshunds, Pugs, Boston Terriers, Miniature Pinschers, Chihuahuas, Maltese, Miniature Schnauzers, Jack Russells, Toy Poodles, Yorkshire Terriers, Lhasa Apsos, Bichons, and Beagles. The larger the breed the least chance of a reaction; the three breeds at the end of susceptibility of the list are Chow Chows, German Shepherds, and Rottweilers.

In the above list the last breed listed for being the most prevalent is the beagle. Personally I know it to be true that this breed is at risk; this was the case of my parent's second beagle, Maxwell. Shortly after he was adopted into the family he had his first vet appointment. Being a young six months in age it was time for his vaccinations. He was neutered just the following month and now Maxwell was due for his shots.

The staff at the veterinarian hospital in Erie was just as any other hospital. Kyle, my father, had taken Maxwell to the appointment where all the usual and customary exams and procedures were done. At the very end of the exam the combination vaccine was given. My father was not given the risks of the combination vaccine, in fact most vets don't refer to the shots in that term. Most veterinarians' just list off the shots that the dogs needs and often don't inform the owner's of the risks. A half-ass consent is obtained with out the full-knowledge of these combo shots and the potential for reactions, especially for small breed of dogs. The combo vaccine was given and the damage was done, unknowingly. According to the bill four vaccines were given at one time.

Within twenty-four hours Maxwell started to have serious reactions. That night he had a seizure and both my parents had taken him to a round-the-clock emergency pet center in town. Kyle and Denise were beside themselves with worry. During the emergency exam the information about the vet appointment earlier that day was passed along to the veterinarian on call. The seizure was a reaction to the combination shot. They were given anti-seizure medications for Max and were told to make a follow-up appointment with his regular vet in the morning.

The one-time seizure passed, but it was not the end of his reactions. In the days following Max had begun to act oddly. He was snipping at the air, running and acting scared, and whining when he looked up at the ceiling. Again, my parents were understandably upset and worried and took

87

him to the vet immediately. Maxwell was suffering from a neurological disorder, caused by the combination vaccine.

Fly-bys is what the condition is called in layman's terms. It is irreversible condition to where Max thinks he sees small black spots (flys, more or less) which hover around him and the thinks that they are attacking him. It is a condition that there is no treatment nor any medications that can suppress the *Flys*. He can be administered a sedative if he is extremely bothered by it, but my parents have never do that to him. Maxwell has found a way to cope when the condition is at its worst. While he fluffs his blankets and hides under them, he often does it to escape the *Flys*; he curls up in his ball of comfort and falls asleep as it is the only way Maxwell knows how to deal with his infliction. He was imposed with this life-long neurological disorder from the reaction of the combination vaccine.

Aside from the several vaccines all in one dose the combination vaccine is composed of live viruses (bacteria), aluminum (adjuvant boosting agent), mercury (preservative), gentocin, antifungal and fungal stats, and proprietary agents. Personally, I have a problem with mercury being used in anything that is injected into the human body. Can anyone say Autism for dogs? Due to the fact that dogs are not human the use of mercury is not prohibited in canine vaccines as it now is in children's vaccines by the FDA and CDC.

Combination vaccines should never be given to any dog, especially to small and medium breeds. For any vaccine weight is the largest factor in putting an animal at risk. Studies have shown that age, dogs from 1.5 to 2.5 years old are at the highest risk along with neutered and spayed dogs also being higher than intact canines. There is no difference shown in reaction risk in pure-bred status, whether the canine is pure bred or mixed all are equally both susceptible to having severe reactions.

The reason that the weight of the dog makes the most difference in whether a reaction may occur does not lie in the live vaccine or bacteria present in the shots, but it comes from the additives. The mercury and aluminum, being used as preservatives and boosting agents, cause the most harm in the one-size-fits-all vaccines by too much of these ingredients being introduced into the canine's body. The vaccines that are given singly, drawn up in the vet's office, and administered by the dog's body weight do not contain as much of the additives and therefore do not pass along as much of those products into the dog's body. Therefore, the single-dose vaccines being spaced apart appropriately and not given all at once does not shock and overdose the dog's body, which limits the percentage for risks and reactions.

Why do veterinarians use the combination vaccines if they pose great risks to our canines? I guess the answer is money. Vet offices save a lot of money by using the one-size-fits-all vaccines, even though it gives canines a higher risk for reactions. The number two reason is convenience. It's a one visit, one poke situation where it involves less time, effort, and thought into providing dogs and their owners with the proper vet care.

So what needs no happen to ensure the safety of our canines? On the large scale the CDC and FDA need to place more rigid guidelines on pet vaccines. They need to limit the amount of additives and, in my opinion, do away all together with the combination vaccines and administer single doses based on weight and age. Is that hoping for too much?

Second, at a more individual level, people should do research into the vaccines that their pets are receiving. Get aware of the risks and reactions and do additional research into your current vet or other vets. Also, some kennels, and groomers try to "bully" dog owners into getting unnecessary vaccines, it is solely up to veterinarians to provide you with this information. Don't allow anyone to do this to you or your dog.

Another alternative is looking into holistic veterinarians. Not all vets are created equal and some out there put wellness, nutrition, and holistic care paramount when working with owners regarding the health care of their dogs. Knowledge is power and making the best informed decision for your dog starts with you.

Information and statistics were obtained from JAMVA (Journal of American Veterinary Medical Association), WSAVA (World Small Animals Veterinarian Association), and other articles referenced.

Cases of Mistreatment

Puppy Mill

Before Jason became a certified groomer and vet assistant he worked at a kennel for Labrador Retriever breeders. He did the kennel work which consisted of feeding, cleaning, and lifting. At first the place seemed ok enough, but the longer he worked there the more it seemed to be like a puppy mill.

In a ranch style home and three outside areas held over two hundred and twenty five Labradors! There were seventy that were kept upstairs and the remainder were in the basement. Almost all of the dogs were kept in crates. The others were grouped and stayed in common areas. The females and puppies were kept in the common areas and all of their male dogs were kept in kennels.

At any given time there were five litters of nursing puppies that were kept in large bin-type areas with their mother until weaning was complete and they were to be sold. The owners/breeders, a mother and her son, charged nine to fifteen hundred for one puppy. Even that price for AKC pure bred dogs was on the extreme side.

I visited the house several times and loved all the dogs, and especially the puppies. People often visited who wanted to see the puppies and purchase them. There were constantly inspectors and lawyers in and out of there as well. Would-be buyers would see the conditions that these dogs were living in and report it to the authorities, good for them. The owner's were also getting slapped with fines left and right, a five thousand dollar fine here and a ten thousand dollar fine there. They griped, but paid them. They complied with all of the warnings and met all of their court dates, but still they were allowed to operate.

The house and grounds constantly smelled of urine and feces. The dogs practically lived in it sometimes. Even with hired help over two hundred dogs is too much, they completely overlooked the health and safety for these animals for the sole purpose of monetary profit. By all means of the definition they are a puppy mill.

None of the dogs were aggressive and all had a good temperament despite the cattle-like conditions. These dogs were kept, boxed, and used for their pedigree. This saddened both Jason and me that puppies and dogs of all ages had to live like this, to be profited and reaped from. Why wouldn't the authorities shut this place down? There were dozens of complaints and the bottom line is the living conditions do not allow much space and the space is not adequately cleaned for the animals. By law each dog is supposed to have a set amount of space and this ranch house does not offer enough space for even a fifth of the amount of dogs that they have.

Jason worked there a total of four months and then he had enough. Besides living conditions the owner's were rude to all of their employees and they had a very high turnover rate. They were not compliant with any of the tax and payroll laws and procedures, or workplace safety for that matter. The only thing that Jason misses about that place is the dogs themselves, especially the puppies. They were all beautiful dogs and would make wonderful pets to their perspective owners despite their upbringing in that deplorable environment.

Demon and Lucky

Jason's employment at the "puppy mill" had been an experience of mixed blessings. As he worked he learned a lot about Labradors and dogs in general. The kennel experience was a plus for him which helped him get the job at the vet hospital as a groomer. As much as there were positives in working there were negatives as well. Even though this business bred the Labradors, it seemed more like a puppy mill.

Some negatives affected him more personally than just the unlivable conditions. These negatives affected his heart. At any given time there were sixty puppies which were to be sold. After working there for two months there was one puppy in particular whom he loved. Jason called him Demon. Though it was a shame that his puppy did not have a name, none of them did. Shortly after birth each puppy was tattooed with a set of letters and numbers on the stomachs. Demon's number was T5438. The "T" must have stood for trouble.

Demon was a strong-willed trouble maker at just six weeks of age. Of his litter he was the biggest and badest of them all. Demon was a yellow lab, but his fur was pure white with blue eyes and yet he had a soft spot for Jason. This little white ball of destruction would constantly escape from his bin and go tearing through the upstairs barking frantically as if to say "I'm free". Occasionally he was crafty enough to get outside in one of the fenced in areas. At one point during his escape to the outside world he ran down the nearby dirt road and terrorized the neighbor's horses. *How could one little puppy cause so much ruckus?* Jason would often think this to himself and smile, he was perfect.

He knew he wanted Demon. He was just like him, a risk-taker and a free spirit. The owner's had never put a collar or leash on a puppy unless they left the property. They had to make an exception for Demon. He was fitted with a purple collar and the pup wanted nothing to do it. Most dogs go through an adjustment period when they first wear a collar. It's bounding and confining. Demon hated it and refused to let up on scratching the collar, it was an obsession. He must have allergic to the bonds of society. Just like Jason.

Jason had asked the owner permission to buy Demon at the discount that they were going to give him. One hundred dollars was much easier to pay than nine hundred dollars. Jason' mistake was that he did not think to get it in writing. It was still a few weeks away until Demon could be adopted and Jason had put his trust in these people. That turned out to be a heart-breaking mistake.

Jason was non-stop excited about getting Demon. He had all the necessary supplies and even special picked out a camo doggie bed for him. A few days before Jason was able to take Demon home the owner's had sold him. It was a day that Jason was working and on his lunch break he always played with Demon. This afternoon a young twenties college-looking blonde walked in and scooped Demon right out of the bin when Jason was playing with him. She didn't say a word to Jason. She held Demon, who struggled intently, and walked up to the owner and said I'll take him. Jason was shocked. She didn't so much as even take any time to play with him or check out any of the other puppies.

"He's not for sale." The owner barked.

Jason had smiled at this. *Victory!* He thought to himself. The woman frowned and said to the owner.

"I'll give you double the price." Her attitude was as rude and condescending as Jason had ever seen.

"That would be eighteen hundred dollars." The owner snippily replied and figured that she would give up, but instead dug in her handbag and pulled out two-thousand dollars in cash. The owner and Jason were both shocked.

"He's yours." The owner replied to the woman and Jason immediately went over to them.

"I paid you for Demon and I was promised." The owner now turned on Jason. "She wants him. You can have another one or I'll give you your money back."

The woman smirked and the owner finished up the paperwork, concluding the sale. Jason was heartbroken and outraged. There was nothing that he could do. He knew he screwed up and should have gotten the deal in writing. He didn't want another puppy. He knew all these puppies as well as he knew himself and he wanted Demon. In two days he would be gone. He hoped he would be treated right in his new home.

Even though this woman had money she had no regard for him. Jason thought.

Jason did his job every day as he was paid to. He already had no respect for the owners by the way they ran their business and took care of the dogs and property and now he had the opposite, only distain for them. He loved the dogs and the puppies so he stayed on and continued his employment there. Someone needed to care for them and look after them. It most certainly was not their owners.

There were several litters of puppies; there was the yellow and white litter, which had Demon and his brothers and sisters, they were ready to leave. The younger litters consisted of a set of yellow and black mixed. There were two sets of black, one chocolate litter, and two red litters. Red is the newest lab color. It had just recently been recognized by the AKC and this breeder had world championship bloodlines which sired all of the red litters. This is why the owners wanted to charge the outrageous amount for the red puppies.

Jason and I thought that all of the red puppies looked similar, but as they got older their personalities added to their uniqueness. Jason had missed Demon and he still held a special place in his heart. There was another puppy that Jason had really taken to as well. Her number was R1149. She was a Red Labrador, but to Jason her name was Lucky. Her left eye was deformed and had cataracts. She was born like that and though she had an undeniable cuteness to her along with a never-give-up attitude. Jason became fond of her and the owners were sure that no one would purchase her due to her eye deformity.

Upon a routine vet visit they had discovered a tumor in Lucky's troubled eye. The vet and owner decided to operate on the eye. Jason and I do commend the owner for taking the action of having the eye operated on and taking the extra effort and care for this one special pup. The owner drove to Cleveland Ohio, which was about a two-hundred mile drive one way. Lucky stayed at a Cleveland vet hospital for two days and was then ready to go back home. The owner knew what the outcome was from the surgery and knew how Jason would react.

Jason came to work the day after Lucky returned and he couldn't wait to see his "little lady", that was her nickname. Jason went to her bin and instantly knew which one was Lucky. She was separated from her litter due to the healing wound and Jason saw the small Elizabethan collar that she was wearing. Jason knelt down and called over to her and she instantly ran to him. As soon as she turned her head enough towards him he saw the stitches and the flattened surface where her eye used to be. The eye was removed during the surgery and Jason cried the moment he saw her. To him she was beautiful and lucky to be alive.

Despite her ordeal, Lucky's disposition was never better. She missed Jason and licked his face rapidly. He picked her up and held her carefully. The owner walked over and said. "She has to heal and have the stitches out in a few weeks, but then she will be yours." "

Thank you so much." Jason replied to her. He carefully set Lucky down and continued with his work. The loss of Demon was replaced by gaining Lucky. He again was happy and ecstatic.

Lucky's return visit and suture removal went well. She was weaned off of pain meds and the area healed nicely. She was more bouncy and beautiful as ever. After she returned back with the breeder she still needed to be watched closely for another week then she could have her permanent home with Jason, myself, and Amber.

Amber and I loved Lucky just as much as Jason and we could hardly wait for the new puppy's arrival in our home. Jason had taken the following weekend off so we could go to our cabin in the mountains. We were both working hard and needed a well-deserved break. The following week we were getting Lucky. This sadly again did not happen. That weekend a couple in their mid-fifties were in to select a Labrador puppy. The owners explained to Jason that the wife was partially and legally blind herself and she fell in love with Lucky. The owner apologized half-heartedly again.

"This is a business and I need to make money." This was her only excuse.

This now happened a second time to him and we were all let down as much as anyone could be let down. Jason now wanted to do nothing with "this business" as his boss had explained it and looked for employment elsewhere. I was as supportive as I could be and luckily he found the grooming position at the vet hospital.

Everything that comes to be happens for a reason. We have tried to accept that philosophy as much as possible. Two little perfect lab puppies that almost were ours, weren't in the end. Jason, Amber, and I all hope that Demon and Lucky have been well taken care of by their new people.

The Unknown Pup –We Call Her Amy

A routine afternoon as the same as any other day, my husband and I went to go pick up our daughter at after-school care. I walked into the school gymnasium and while Amber got her coat and book bag I chatted with Kathy, the after care supervisor, for a minute as I did everyday. Upon returning to the car I walked around to the rear side and Amber smiled and waved at Jason who was in the driver's seat. Just as I opened the back door for Amber I was startled by a fast moving visitor. As soon as I saw the swiftly moving dog it jumped up in my arms. I was shocked, by her sudden presence for one, and also I never had a dog jump up in my arms before.

I rapidly took in the dog seeing that it was a Jack Russell puppy. Jason and Amber both saw what happened and joined me on the side of the car with the dog. I held the puppy inventorying it while it shook and shivered. It was mid-December and the small dog must have been only four or five months old. Jason held the dog and as inconspicuously as possible had determined it was a girl. Of course, Amber was ecstatic and wanted to keep her. She had no collar and there was no one else around. Jason held her while I went back into the school to see if any of the workers may have known who the dog belonged to. Kathy said the house just east of the school on top the hill had a lot of dogs. She said she had seen a few dogs running around the school parking lot from time to time.

I exited the building again and went back out the car. Amber and Jason were ogling over the pretty and petite terrier pup. Amber insisted that the new puppy and Baby Girl would be best friends so we should keep her. I had told Jason what Kathy had said and he decided to take her up to the house to see if she belonged to them. By now the snow flurries had started and Jason rushed off eager to find the puppy shelter before the temperatures dropped even more. He crossed the school property and went up the hill with her in his arms.

Jason got to the top of the hill and walked along the drive to the walkway. The house was a two-story brick with a large picture window in the front and a long privacy fence. He passed in front of the window he noticed there were no curtains and had seen a few dogs inside. He stopped and knocked on the front door. It took a minute, but a woman opened the door and rudely said "Yea?"

She was in her mid-thirties, had a cigarette in her mouth, and a hand on her hip. Jason could see her attitude instantly and did not like it. He noticed all the dogs in the living room, maybe eight or nine total.

"My family found this dog down by the school and one of the workers thought it may be yours." Jason candidly asked in hopes that she would say *no*.

What happened next shocked Jason to his core. She said. "Yea! It's mine." She reached out and forcefully grabbed the puppy out of Jason's arms. She had ignorantly thrown the dog on the floor then slammed the front door shut. There was no thank you given or any amount of concern for the dog that came from this woman. He peered through the picture window once more and the puppy was on the floor mingling with all the other dogs. The other dogs were Jack Russells, Beagles, and Bassett Hounds. He did feel that the dog belonged to these people, but now wished he hadn't returned it.

He was angered and felt awful as he walked back down the hill and returned to the car with no puppy. Jason got back in the car and shook off the remained of the snow which accumulated on him. I could see his expression and asked what happened. He explained and knew what my reaction would be, absolute disgust.

"If I lost a dog and someone returned it to me I would at least say 'thank you'!" I was yelling in the car, but not at Jason or Amber. The situation was unbelievable. These owners showed a complete lack of concern for their dogs. We drove off towards home saddened, only talking about what had just happen.

I was outraged. If this woman didn't want or care about the puppy we would gladly take it and care for it. We regretted what we did even though it was the right thing. Jason and I both agreed that if we could re-do that situation that we would have kept the dog. It would have been far better off being happy and cared for by our family versus that lady. We both wanted to go back to the house, but didn't.

The hard part of all of this was explaining the situation to Amber. She had been there and was aware of the situation. We had explained to her that even though sometimes you do the right thing it doesn't feel right or turn out right. We hope that this woman gets her act together and takes proper care of her dogs. We also decided that if we ever saw the dog again running around with no collar that we would take her in. Amber commented that if it was up to her she would have bought the puppy a pink collar and name her Amy.

Angel

The worst case of animal neglect and mistreatment I'd encountered was in 2005. A co-worker of mine, Vanessa, had told me about her sister, Natalie who had a three-year old smooth collie that she owned but did not want.

From what Vanessa had told me, Natalie was in her mid-forties. Both she and her sister had a very hard life growing up and had Natalie had gotten in trouble at a young age with men, drugs, and the law. She lived in Ohio with her boyfriend and the collie, which lived outside and was chained to a shed. The collie did not even have a name and at first I referred to her as "no name". She was occasionally fed and given water, but was shunned from all human interaction. She has spent the better part of her life living in these conditions.

Vanessa did not defend nor condone her sister, after all they were sisters, but Vanessa wanted to see the collie go to a good home and at the time I was looking for another dog to be a companion to Rocky. Vanessa brought in pictures, which did not do any justice showing the true living conditions and shape that the collie was in, in fact they were worse. I made arrangements with Vanessa, she and Natalie were going to drive to my home from Ohio and bring the dog with them.

The two sisters, along with the collie, arrived mid-afternoon on a fall Saturday. Amber was at her best friend's birthday party and I had put Rocky away in the bedroom so I could inventory the incoming dog without too much distraction. They arrived and brought "no name" into my backyard. After a brief introduction and meeting Natalie I could see that she had no regard for herself, let alone a dog.

The collie had the most awful coat I had ever seen on a dog. She looked like a matted dirty and smelly lion. The fur was long and unkempt and looked as if there were dread locks all over her. She had a wonderful affectionate personality and was not timid or scared. She took instantly to me and I liked her in return. I held back with everything that I had. I wanted to curse and scream at this woman for mistreating her dog. I kept my cool and agreed to take the collie. From looking at her she had never been groomed or bathed once in her three years of her life. She was going to be a lot of work, but that did not bother me. I had daggers for this woman in my heart and thankfully they did not stay long.

Natalie did not care who took the dog and walked towards the car in my mid-sentence and I was beyond livid with her attitude. I spoke with Vanessa for another minute or two and thanked her for the dog. They were gone and I had work to do.

"No name" liked running around my fenced-in yard. I brought out a bowl of food and water for her, which she ate quickly. The vet office I took Rocky to was also an animal hospital and they were open on Saturdays. I called immediately and explained the situation then for the following week I had a vet and grooming appointment scheduled. I knew that it would be a long and tiresome day as the collie needed a lot of work.

I needed to think of a name, but before that I attempted to do some grooming myself. "No name" was willing but cautious. I was able to clip her talon-like nails and cut some of her long fur. It was time consuming and arduous. She was washed and conditioned, but still smelled and the fur was still way too long. Grooming would have to wait until the beginning of the following week. She stayed outside most of the day since the weather was fair and at night she stayed in the basement.

I had done a slow introduction with her and Rocky. They both liked each other and didn't bark; they only sniffed and played. That was most pleasing that the two dogs would get along. Rocky was intrigued with her farm-smelling fur. Amber also loved our new dog. Amber was young at the time, in kindergarten, and loved the idea of having two dogs. She knew that the dog was going to be all cleaned up and taken care of at the vet office in a few days and that seemed acceptable to her. For a young child she was very receptive to the collie's condition and was happy that we were going to keep her and care for her.

It was Tuesday, appointment day. Though I explained to the staff on the phone about the dog's physical appearance they were not prepared and were just as shocked as I was when I first saw her. They didn't know whether to start with the grooming or the vet exam and it seemed that neither wanted to go first. Finally the vet saw her. He was shocked at her state and he and the staff commended me for taking her in. I wanted above all to make sure that she was ok physically and was healthy.

She had her shots and tests were done. They found a worm parasite and gave her a med supply which would take care of it. Besides that she was in perfect health besides the malnourishment. She was about fifteen pounds underweight, but that would be rectified fairly quickly as she was hungry and ate a lot. I fed her the same dog food as I gave Rocky. It was a high-end dog food that was optimum for their health, she adjusted well to it and I was pleased that overall she was in excellent health.

Next came the grooming, which was the hardest and most tedious part of the visit. They were behind and said it would be a few hours so I left her in capable hands and did some errands. When I returned I had a brand new looking dog waiting for me. I was pleasantly surprised and the staff was giving each other kudos for a job well done. Her horrendous coat was gone and a soft shiny light-colored coat was brought out on her and she was clipped to perfection. She looked so skinny I could barely believe it was the same dog. The fur was so bad that they cut it extremely short, which was fine. She smelled fabulous and looked spectacular.

Upon leaving I thanked the staff several times over and I left with a very new, very pretty, very expensive dog. The bill was quite large, but worth it. I never liked spending money on myself, but I didn't mind spending it on my four-legged friends. I always thought of it as money well spent.

The collie was quite pleased with herself as well and now the last task was to pick out a name. I needed something that fit well and perhaps the best name of all for her was Angel. Upon bringing Angel home Rocky also did a double-take he smelled her thoroughly, but in the end was happy she was the same dog only improved. Rocky and Angel were quite a pair. Nearly the same age they loved to romp around the yard together and played endlessly.

I had brought pics in to show Vanessa what Angel had looked like after her grooming and told her how well she was adjusting to her new home. Vanessa was ecstatic that the collie now had a good home and knew that I would be just that person to provide that stability for the dog.

As Angel adjusted to the home environment she was no longer timid. A confident self emerged and she was sure of her new family and her surroundings. Between the two canines she asserted herself as the alpha dog of the pack and

Rocky willingly agreed. He was a smitten with her and though he was a confident leader when it came to search and rescue at home he let Angel be in charge and took the submissive role. I guess this is also found and true in some human relationships.

Even though I was Angel's angel having rescued her from a mistreated home she was in return our angel as she completed our family.

Societal & Vet Responsibilities

Melamine Pet Food Crisis – Part Two

"Perky come here!" Sandy cheerfully called out as she crawled around on the living room floor. She was on her hands and knees on the tan carpet looking behind all of the forest-green upholstered furniture looking for her best friend Perky, a Scottish terrier. Both Sandy and Perky were six years old, only separated by two months.

Being curious and having a frowning expression Sandy had thought. *Where are you Perky?* Sandy thought. Their favorite game to play together was peek-a-boo. Besides age the pair had a lot in common: they each had black hair, liked the color pink (Perky often donned a pink and white plaid sweater), and they both disliked cats.

"There you are Perky." Sandy said and smiled as she rounded the corner of the loveseat. Sandy could see the small black dog's tail, legs, and part of the sweater. The rest of Perky was hidden under the couch.

"Got 'ya!" Sandy called out when she put her small hand on Perky's back and petted her. Perky did not move.

What's wrong with Perky? The dog still did not move and Sandy was now worried, though she did not show it. Sandy was not able to pull the dog out because of the positioning of Perky under the couch with the wall and end table nearby. She got up off the floor and hurried into the kitchen to retrieve her mother.

"Mom!" Sandy cried out as the entered the kitchen. "There's something wrong with Perky."

The phone at their house rang later that evening. It was Sandy's father; he had taken Perky to the veterinarian office after Sandy and her mother had found Perky unconscious on the floor.

"Is she ok..." Becky, Sandy's mother, asked with fear and concern as her voice trailed off. Her husband Fred sighed heavily on the phone.

"She's in bad shape, but she's still alive. How's Sandy doing?" He inquired.

She answered warily. "She's ok. Worried, but doing alright. What caused Perky to collapse?" Becky asked but was afraid of the answer.

"Well, her kidneys aren't working right. That's what all the tests show. Perky is going stay overnight and I will be home as soon as I can." Each said that they loved each other and Fred asked if she would keep their daughter in good spirits. In turn, Becky had done her best, but the fact that Perky was not at home with Sandy was upsetting.

Perky stayed at the Verona Valley Vet. Hospital and the blood tests were re-run. The vets on staff all consulted about Perky's case. She was the fourth canine to come in the vet's office in two weeks with kidney problems.

"There must be something in the water." One of the vets had half-heartedly joked. It was summer of 2007 when vets all over the country had recognized the cases of kidney disease and failure and the pieces were slowly coming together, but only on a primary level.

Perky was hospitalized for three days. She was given several meds and the regimens had worked as best they could. Her kidney's were slightly damaged, but were not in failure to Perky's benefit. Perky had been lucky by all costs and her family was even more relieved. Sandy was by far relieved the most, because her best friend and companion, Perky, was home. Despite surviving Perky was never quite was the same; she was always on one med or another one. Occasionally the family volunteered to have Perky try a new experimental treatments and hoped for a breakthrough. Typically the regimens did not have either a positive or negative effect as Perky had remained continually stable. All the while canines and felines all of the United States were dying of kidney failure or had various stages of kidney disease. Perky was among the luckiest.

The CDC had drawn their conclusions and parallels with the high amount of the kidney cases reported all around the country. They knew there was a major problem and connected all of the dots. Finally the warnings and recalls were issued for the tainted pet products. The CDC in this case of Melamine reminds me of how they handled the Autism epidemic over the last decade and a half. A record number of infants and children were diagnosed with Autism and the majority was administered vaccines, though the government adamantly denies vaccines are one cause to Autism, despite any evidence. I specifically remember the hearings of the FDA and the legislature. A televised hearing included brash accusations from a state senator whose grandson was administered a vaccine and immediately went into regression and soon after he was diagnosed with Autism. Mercury was added to children's vaccines and used as a "preservative" just as Melamine was used a "preservative" in pet foods.

Both the Melamine and mercury poisonings occurred for long periods of time until the problems presented themselves in large numbers. In both instances I have been personally and negatively affected by the uses of the so-called "preservatives". My child has autism from the mercury and my first dog passed away from the Melamine. I am not against our government in any fashion, but it is convenient how they like to say "Sorry", but do very little and leave behind the heart-breaking relics of their mistakes. These oversights should never have occurred. Proper monitoring guidelines need to be in place before products are produced, distributed, and sold. Responsibility is a factor that should be shared by all and not just a lump that was swept under the carpet and left. In the Melamine Pet Food Crisis the canines, felines, and their owners have suffered the ill effects of Loss-sponsibility.

Overcoming Autism

When my daughter, Amber, was eighteen months old she was diagnosed with Autism Spectrum Disorder being moderate to severe in various symptoms. It was devastating and I knew the venture ahead would be difficult.

I noticed the signs immediately after her twelve month booster shots. She had regressed in her speech and learning and had focal-point seizures. I brought it to the attention of her doctor right away. Appointments were set up and she had three therapists assigned to her even before the initial diagnosis was given. Tests and observations were completed and scaled; after the heart-wrenching diagnosis and label was applied she was accepted to a specialized preschool program for Autistic children.

When Amber was about two years old and just starting the preschool program I had decided to get a dog. Upon doing research I was interested in and decided upon Labrador retrievers. They are excellent with children, and do all sorts of therapy dog work and search and rescue work. I wanted a dog that would stimulate Amber intellectually and one that I could train to do volunteer work with. Upon searching shelters in the area I found a four month old black lab and Rottwilier mix. I loved his demeanor and temperament, not to mention how cute he was.

Amber was astounded with him as well. I could see her face light up and her little brain thinking. Not only did I do everything for my daughter to help overcome this terrible thing that happened to her, but I enlisted the help of friends and family as well. Rocky was no exception to the list, in fact, he was a large part. She physically wanted to play with Rocky, it had helped her gross motor skills. Amber wanted to pet Rocky and stroke his fur, fine motor skills were worked on and improved as well.

The area most progressed area for her was her speech, was went from normal to non-existent was now making a comeback. She loved this dog; she loved playing and reading to him. Me, Amber, and Rocky were often sitting on the couch or floor we were all huddled around a book constantly. At preschool they had all types of educational toys, peer interaction, and the most trained Autism-specialized personnel, but the one thing I stressed educationally when I was at home with Amber was books. I myself love reading and I wanted to pass that along to my daughter no matter what her abilities or disabilities were.

It worked. She started out slow first by liking looking at the pictures and colors in the books. Even though it took her a while to speak again she would get books and bring them to me. Eventually she made sounds. She loved talking to Rocky. It was somewhat gibberish and only Amber knew what she was saying but still sounds were spoken, then eventually words developed. Amber read to Rocky and in time she was speaking and reading slowly yet methodically.

At one of the check-ups with the psychologist, the same whom first diagnosed Amber, had commented about the progress she was making both at preschool and at home. Being a toddler she went from having three therapists down to one, a speech pathologist. Even still, several years later Amber still has a speech therapist, but meets her goals expectantly. I had told the psychologist about getting a dog and that Amber likes to read to him. He had commended me for the choice in breed and encouraging Amber to read through an effective and creative pathway, Rocky.

The preschool program had allowed Amber to start preschool a year early instead of waiting, which had also helped in her success. In all she had four years of the specialized preschool program and she had made tremendous progress throughout that time. Even now, she has been retested and due to a numbers scale she now has the mildest form of Autism on the spectrum. She does not even currently show signs or symptoms of her label, but the label remains per psychiatrists.

Former therapists, teachers, and assistants from that time period whom I run across every now and then see

Amber and how much she has progressed and overcome her diagnosis and they can barely believe that it is the same girl. I give them credit where credit it due as well as myself and my parents whom never let this "diagnosis" overcome any of us, let alone Amber. Rocky had done his part and helped incredibly; he just never even knew it. Just his presence of him being there was motivation for her. Even though challenges remain she has done the unbelievably well by doing her best to overcome Autism.

A Pup's Life Cut Short

Mac, a one-year old Saint Bernard puppy went for his routine grooming appointment at the Verona Valley Veterinarian Hospital. He was a whopping seventy-five pounds and was full of energy, and fur. Manny, a groomer, vet assistant, and co-worker of Jason was doing Mac's grooming one Friday morning. Mac was being extra pampered and was getting "the works".

Manny loved Mac, as Saint Bernard's were his favorite breed of dog. Mac was washed, dried, clipped, and combed; he loved every minute of it. "Here you go boy." Manny said. For the finishing touch he tied a royal and navy blue bandana around Mac's neck, as his owner, Sally, requested blue for Mac. Sally, an elderly woman, had been bringing Mac there for of his vet care and grooming since she had gotten him. All of the staff liked Mac as he was a joy to be around.

Mac had the traditional dark and light brown coloring in large varied patches on his white coat. His most distinguishing feature was a white upside-down triangle on his forehead that tipped out on his nose. He was beautiful and had a good temperament. Manny was a lover of large dog breeds.

"The bigger, the better." He always said and with Saint Bernard's being the biggest, he loved them the most. After Manny was finished he secured Mac in a kennel; Sally was due to pick him up any minute. He liked to finish early with the dogs, but he took a few extra minutes to play with Mac.

"Manny! Ms. Sally is here." Marie, the receptionist, yelled into the grooming area.

"Ok boy. Time to go home." Manny opened the large kennel door and hooked Mac's leash on his collar. Mac gave one him one more lick on the face for the road and Manny laughed. Manny had brought Mac out to the lobby to find Sally waiting. The elderly woman was timely and also in a hurry. She paid for the services, took his leash, and left abruptly. "Thank you." She said to Manny before she left. She lived alone in a large house in a fancy area of Pittsburgh.

No one at the vet and grooming office could figure why an elderly lady like her had chosen such a large dog to care for. The seventy-five pound pooch pulled Sally out the door and through the parking lot. Sally was maybe sixty years old and she could accidentally be hurt by Mac's size. He could bump her and she could fall with ease. It remained a mystery, but the next few grooming appointments for the day were ready and Manny had other dogs to tend to.

The weekend passed quickly. Manny worked all day Saturday, but was off on Sunday. Monday's were always busy and Manny had a full schedule to groom forty dogs.

"Another Monday." He said to himself while scanning the list for dogs that he knew. He saw that he recognized at least half the names and he smiled. Despite being busy it would be a good day.

Patrice, the grooming supervisor came in around nine every morning. She was making her rounds and talked to one of the vets on the hospital side of the building. Manny was washing a Mastiff when Patrice came over into the grooming area and gave Manny the bad news.

"Do you remember that Saint Bernard puppy from Friday?" Patrice asked him.

"Yes. Why?" Manny didn't know why she was asking.

"Well, the owner just brought him in and they are going to put him to sleep."

"What?! Why?" Manny asked and was confused. He finished rinsing off the Mastiff, shut the water off quickly, dried his hands, and secured the Mastiff in a kennel.

Patrice continued. "I guess he snipped at her over the weekend and now she wants him to be put down." Manny's brow was arched and eyes narrowed. He tried not to show his anger, but still fumed.

"He's a puppy and only a year old. Of course, he may snip, but he isn't aggressive." By now, Manny and Patrice left the grooming area and walked over to the veterinarian side of the building. Patrice was just was upset, but she was a manager and though she spoke her mind on several matters often, she also had to watch her temper. Things like this outraged her more than Manny would ever know.

They went to the reception area and asked when Mac was going to be put to sleep.

"In about fifteen minutes or so." May, the vet receptionist, had replied. Manny then thought to himself. "I have to do something about this."

Patrice was paged for a phone call, before she went to her office she said to Manny.

"Please don't go overboard on this." He nodded and looked for Dr. Berrly, the vet who was scheduled to put Mac down. After a few minutes of searching the building he found Dr. Berrly. He was an average sized man in his fifties with thinning hair and glasses.

"Dr. Berrly I'm glad I found you. I heard that they are putting Mac, the Saint Bernard puppy down in a few minutes."

Dr. Berrly replied. "Yes Manny. I am."

"Why? How can this be allowed to happen?" Manny was now getting desperate. He thought that if this woman didn't want the puppy then someone else gladly would care for him."

Dr. Berrly responded in absence. "I don't want to, but it's my job."

He could see that Manny was upset and he decided to explain further, even though he didn't have to.

"Manny. Sally Enders brought Mac in and said that he snipped at her once this weekend and now she doesn't want him and even worse than that she wants him put to sleep. I tried to reason with her and brought it to the owner's attention, but Ms. Enders is adamant about it she doesn't feel safe with him."

Manny asked in return. "Can the Humane Society, a rescue group, or anyone else take him in until a better home is found?" "Dr. Berrly smiled and tried to put Manny at ease, but it didn't work.

"Manny. The real reason that Ms. Enders can get away with this... is money. She called the owners and told them that she would pay the vet hospital three times as much as what the normal fee is to put him down." Manny's jaw dropped at least an inch.

"What!" Now he was pissed off. "This old lady thinks she can throw money around and kill her dog?!" He was not trying to yell at the doctor, it was not his fault, but it all slipped away from him. Dr. Berrly said to Manny.

"Please do your best to control yourself. I know it's unfair and we are not able to control this."

"Sorry. Thank you doctor." Manny left the room in haste and went out to the waiting room.

While walking a jumbling process of all his thoughts bounced around in his head. He knew he would get written up or maybe even lose his job, but his opinion would be heard and someone had to fight for this puppy's rights. He neared the waiting room and saw Ms. Enders sitting there near a window seat looking at a dog magazine. Most likely Mac was in a holding kennel. He boiled inside and walked right up to Sally Enders.

"Ms. Enders can I have a word with you." Manny said quickly and forcefully. She recognized him immediately and set the periodical down on the table next to her.

"Sure Manny." Manny sat down next to her and wasted no time.

"I've heard why you have brought Mac in today. To be put down. Is that true?"

He hoped she would have changed her mind.

"He snipped at me and I am not going to tolerate that behavior." Her cooperative behavior had become defensive now. The staff up until now just ignored her and said only the minimum amount, but now she was being challenged.

"He's just barely one year old. He's still going to be a puppy for six more months. He's not aggressive Ms. Enders." She was now just as mad as him.

"My decision stands. Now leave." She made a waving away hand gesture to him and selected another dog magazine. She had to sit there and was not able to leave until Mac had passed and both she and the doctor needed to verify it. She did not want to be in the exam room when Mac was given the lethal injection. She would sign a form or two, write out a large check, and leave.

"This is wrong!" Manny stood up and raised his voice. He wanted all of the other pet owners to hear what he was saying.

"You are making the vets put your one year old puppy to sleep because you want to be a bitch! Dog killer!"

Everyone looked up in surprise, even the workers, and everyone stared at her and talked amongst themselves.

"How dare you!" She hollered in return, but Manny was already walking back towards the grooming department and was approaching Patrice. "I spoke my opinion and whatever happens will happen."

Patrice only nodded and Manny returned to washing the last dog on his list for the morning. This one was also a Saint Bernard and Manny was silent and cried for a few minutes to himself. Someone had to stand up for Mac no matter what the consequences were.

Forty-five minutes passed. Manny was done with the last dog. No one had come over from the vet side or had said anything to him for that matter. He figured that they were done with Mac and Ms. Sally was gone as well.

"Anything else Patrice?" He asked.

She gave him a sympathetic smile and said."We're good for today. You can punch out if you want. Are you going to be in tomorrow?" Patrice had asked him hoping that he wasn't too extremely upset.

"Yes I will." He replied.

"You are brave." Patrice said. "I'm glad that someone put her in her place. Don't worry, you won't be written up or anything." Manny nodded and was relieved. Manny had punched his time sheet and got his coat and keys and was getting ready to leave when Patrice added one more comment. "You gave it your best try and I really commend you for it. I'm sorry that it didn't work out for Mac." Manny acknowledged and thanked her again for her support, then he left somberly.

Not All Vets Are Created Equal

Equality and optimum veterinarian care and service are what every pet owner wants and deserves. Unfortunately, that is not the world we live in. Veterinarians and vet offices are required to follow certain presets which allow for the minimum quality of care. Ethics are a number one priority, some vet offices excel in quality and some struggle to meet standards. Everything else seems to be subjective.

America is a country of diversity and freedom of choice. This is one attribute which makes the United States great, but on the same hand ethics, in any type of business, can fall by the wayside. Supreme service should be paramount, yet capitalism and greed are often replacements. Companies all over the United States are guilty of this, putting money first and people second. Veterinarian offices are no exception and in addition to people being failed by capitalism, so are their pets.

The standard of care at the Verona Valley Vet Hospital is one of the best that I have seen. They are a highly respectable organization that holds ethics at the top of their priorities. This vet hospital is ranked among the top, as it should be. There are approximately thirty-five veterinarian hospitals in Pittsburgh and the surrounding area. This includes the central, north, south, east, and west regions.

Verona Valley has been in business for the last thirty years. Recently, the owner, seventy-eight year old Madeline, had passed away from breast cancer. From the time she was diagnosed until she passed only consisted of a short span of three weeks. Her husband, Carmen, has been involved in the administration of the vet hospital for the last ten years. Immediately upon Madeline's passing, Carmen had made a statement to the staff that the hospital would be sold. He half-heartedly reassured the staff of fifty employees that no changes would be made. Being concerned and worried the staff works just as hard as they always have. Day in and day out they provide the best possible care to their patients and clients. Of all the regions, the north region has the most vet hospitals, twelve in all. Verona Valley is the most dignified vet hospital of the group.

A distressed dog owner had switched vet care from Greenview, central region, to Verona Valley, north region following an incorrectly performed surgical procedure.

The surgery was to elongate a contracted muscle in the snout of a Weimarner, Dutchess. The five-year old Dutchess was owned by Yena. Yena had been bringing Dutchess to the Greenview Veterinarian Care Center since she was a puppy. The contracted muscle had been bothering Dutchess for six months; it was diagnosed as a neurological condition with a physical deformity. Muscle relaxation medications along with physical therapy were tried, but failed. The vet had suggested a surgical procedure to elongate the contracted muscle. The prognosis of the procedure would be to eliminate the pain and to correct the

118

deformity by realigning the muscle. This was their best course of action and Yena had agreed to the plan. Her Dutchess was in pain and wanted to rectify her ailment as soon as possible.

Upon completion of the surgery, Yena was perplexed when the vet surgeon had explained that the muscle was abnormally longer than it should have been and was connected to the right eye. The vet surgeon had seen the stress that the muscle was putting on the eye, and without consulting Yena, he had removed the right eye.

"Why was I not even told about this or asked my wishes?!" She was horrified about the course of action that was taken and in response she shouted due to the surge of panic and fear because that the choice was made without her knowledge. It was a choice that was made, by Yena's account, which now caused further harm to the dog.

"If I knew you were going to remove her eye I never would have let you do the surgery on her!" Yena continued to express her opinion which had fallen on the vet surgeon's deaf ears. To Yena he seemed brash and barked almost as much as the dogs there did. Yena was understandably upset that her wishes were ignored and the vets now showed no concern for her or her dog.

"You can get a list of visitation times from the front desk, along with the bill." The vet surgeon had distantly said to Yena. The red flames of anger were coming off of her in sheets as she tried to contain her emotions.

"She should be ready to go home in a day or two." He finished, abruptly turned with clipboard in hand and walked down the hall.

The daggers were drawn in Yena's hazel eyes which clashed imposingly with her dark brown and graying mixed hair. She marched up to the closest vet tech and explained her concerns. The vet tech, Mary, was very understanding and kind and asked Yena to take a seat. Nearly an hour later Yena was able to see Dutchess in recovery. Those hazel eyes were now enlarged with tears as she surveyed her dog's face. Dutchess was still sedated, but doing well; the bandage and gauze covered the eye socket and partial snout patch. It was stained with iodine and drying blood. The sutures and stitches could also be seen at an angle with fresh blood covering.

"Take care Dutchess." She cried quietly and placed her hand on Dutchess's shoulder while she softly petted the short, soft, gray fur. She admired Dutchess's strength and at that moment hated her involvement in this, in trusting those people.

"I'll come back later and see you." She whispered softly and left the recovery area.

Upon exiting the vet hospital Yena had gotten out her cell phone, wiped her eyes, and placed a call; it was to her lawyer. *Dogs have rights too.* Yena thought as the call connected. She sat in her vehicle and explained the situation and what had happened. Her lawyer, of course, was appalled and was going to prepare the legal papers immediately for when Dutchess would be released. The lawyer happily agreed to be there when Yena was to pick her up.

Greenview, being centrally located downtown was only two blocks from where she worked. Yena worked on the sixteenth floor of a very successful insurance agency in a towering Three-Rivers skyscraper. Greenview was convenient; she was able to drop-off and pick-up Dutchess around her work schedule. It seemed like a decent enough place, but now she had enough of it. She wanted a vet hospital closer to home, especially now, and had to find one immediately.

Yena had heard praise about Verona Valley, which was half a mile from her home on the north side of Pittsburgh. Verona Valley was more expensive, but now money did not matter to her. She was not going to compromise the care of her dog ever again. Money was not an issue since her job afforded her a three-story house in an exquisite suburb. *Yes.* She thought. *Verona Valley is the place.* In addition to a vet hospital, they have the number one grooming salon in the city as well as a pet hotel. Several players for the Pittsburgh Steelers bring their pets there and occasionally a debutant of some sort will have his/her cat or dog dropped off in a limo at the veterinarian facility.

Greenview had wrongly and forcefully removed Dutchess's eye. They were victims of reckless malpractice and something was going to be done about it. She was going to fight for her rights and her dog's rights in order to hopefully prevent anymore pets and owners from going through a similar situation at Greenview. Revenge and money were not her motives for filing the lawsuit; it was justice for the wronged pets and their owners. This was her choice and she made her second phone call to set up an appointment. Dutchess deserved better – the best, and it was Verona Valley.

Dr. Berrly was the staff veterinarian and Dutchess was his first appointment of the day. He was made aware of the situation beforehand and read through the medical chart that was sent over from Greenview. He leafed through his notes in an exam room.

"She was just released yesterday?" He looked up and frowned. Yena nodded while she sat across the room from him.

"Yes. I needed to get her out of there as soon as she was strong enough." Dr. Berryly did a standard exam. He noticed Dutchess's well-mannered disposition despite the pain she has been in.

That morning Yena had changed the dressing accordingly and the sutures were healing. She was instructed to keep the gauzes fresh and changed. The Elizabethan collar was removed for the exam, though Dutchess did not pull or tug on the bandage much, the collar wasn't even needed, it was more of a medical formality. Dr. Berrly removed the bandage and slid over on the rolling stool right up to Dutchess's face. With ample light and a magnifier he studied the stitches of the surgical area. Both Yena and Amber Russell, the vet student, stood on either side of Dutchess to prevent her from moving. Dutchess was quite content on the pain meds as she didn't want to go anywhere or do much of anything.

"It's all healing nicely. That's good news." He slid back and removed the white rubber gloves and pitched them towards the trash, both made it in the rim. "I know they messed up in the first place and she was adversely affected by the mistake, but she is healing just fine and I think she will adjust just fine." Dr. Berrly had candidly spoken to the owner about her dog's condition.

Yena was relieved and yet felt betrayed, not at anything that the doctor had done or said during the exam specifically, but a small part of her wanted Dr. Berrly to verbally bash the other vet hospital for their mistake and this did not happen. The doctor continued looking through the chart while Amber took Dutchess's stats and recorded them.

"The medication all seems to be in order and is helping so no need to change that." He commented somewhat to himself, but spoke loud enough for Yena to hear and scribbled some more notes. "Ok then. Do you have any questions for me?" He asked her. They finished the exam and gave all of the usual post-op directions, which was basically the same care which has been provided to Dutchess for the last few days.

Yena was very impressed with the doctor and the staff. She liked their professionalism and the facility itself. The building and its offices, virtually every area, was immaculate and she was not disappointed in the least with Verona Valley. She had a follow-up appointment in a week when the gauze and Elizabethan collar would be removed. In the mean time Yena was taking Dutchess home; they were both relieved and relaxed.

She let her attorney handle Greenview, and no longer sought retribution. If there would be any monetary gain she planned on donating it to shelters, ASPCA, and various vet institutions for canine diseases research. Yena had plans this weekend. Saturday she was going to the Humane Society to do some volunteering and Sunday she was going to attend the AKC dog show in Pittsburgh. Dutchess has made such a large impact on Yena's life that she has taken a fanatic interest in dogs and is doing what she can on her behalf to help dogs and their owners.

Literary

Tabitha

Tabitha preferred to be alone most of the time. She lived with her fiancé Henry, who was five years younger than her. Henry decided that on her thirty-fifth birthday he would surprise Tabitha with a puppy. To Tabitha, her birthday was just another day and this year it was a rainy and cold April day.

Henry and Tabitha had lived in a two bedroom mobile home with a modest backyard. Since Tabitha had lots of time on her hands she decided that this year she would start a garden. Her mother always had a large vegetable garden when she was growing up. Tabitha preferred eating veggies to meats; though she was not a "vegetarian" per se. Tabitha also thought it would be a good idea for them to save money since over the last two years, ever since she met Henry, there seemed to be a black cloud of bad luck that followed them.

The bad luck didn't bother Henry much. He was used to it as he had a very hard life growing up and through his adulthood. Tabitha on the other hand did not and was not accustomed to having a hard life. She had been a computer programmer and worked at a software company for six years before being laid off. Henry had worked in construction and doing general labor, so when things were good they were good and when things were bad they were bad.

The economy was also bad. It was the year that the younger president Bush left office and Obama came into office. The country was adjusting and certain economic areas continued to decline. The large company that Tabitha had worked for was bailed out by the government. Henry and Tabitha owned a house together and were also victims of the housing foreclosure crisis, mostly in part from her job loss, it was heart breaking for the both of them.

Since Tabitha was still on her "break from working" she kept busy as much as possible. She had plans for her garden and was taking both English and writing courses through a community college. Her tuition was paid through federal and state grants and she did not have to pay anything out of pocket. This was one thing that made Tabitha happy and gave her a goal.

She often sat alone writing. Henry was often at work or out with his friends. Since he was younger and had younger friends Tabitha did not have much in common with most of them. Sometimes she'd go out with them as a group, but lately preferred staying at home.

Her and Henry dated for a few years and now were engaged. They wanted a simple ceremony with just them and a pastor at a beach, but her mother wanted to have a large ceremony, which Tabitha was not in favor of at first. In the past Henry had been a player. He had a roving eye, which he still had and Tabitha knew it. She was madly in love with him, but she still sometimes did not trust him. Henry was equally not trusting in Tabitha. She had been in a few bad relationships and reluctantly went back to the same man who was never faithful to her. Henry and Tabitha both had issues with their past and their relationship was cumbersome at times.

Tabitha's birthday was on a Thursday and Henry usually worked late of Thursdays. Friday's however he only worked half days and they decided to celebrate her birthday then. The weather was also going to be nicer according to the forecast.

On Friday morning Tabitha had worn her oldest jeans and sweat shirt and got prepped to work in her garden. She went out to the shed and gathered up a bunch of tools. She worked outside for a few hours, taking breaks as needed, then Henry pulled up in the driveway. He parked the car and saw her working. She was digging up the dirt around one of the trees in the back of the yard. He got out of the car and to himself admired her slender figure and blonde hair as he started to walk towards her.

She was not afraid to get dirty, this was one of the things that Henry liked best about her. She looked over and smiled and waved at Henry. He was walking across the backyard carrying his coffee mug and newspaper. As he walked he let out a whistle. She smiled, but didn't do more than that. She did not see herself that way, but Henry always did.

"What are you up to gorgeous?" He asked her.

"Planting the Giant Pansy and Snap Dragon seeds that my mom got us for Easter". She replied back to him without looking up. She was nearly done and wanted to finish. She smoothed the dirt around the sowed seeds and covered up them up meticulously. All she had to do was water them and she'd be done with that would-be flower bed.

She wiped the dirt off her gloves and he helped her up. "Hi honey." She said and kissed him.

"Hello yourself." He winked and he liked the fact that she was covered in dirt.

She brushed off his comment and asked him. "So what's the newspaper for?"

She found it curious as he almost never read the paper. "Helping the boss look through the 'ads for bid' section'. He wants to take on more business."

"That's good." She responded, but she did not know that it was a lie. He had bought the newspaper for a more important and more specific reason than that.

"I'm going to stay out for a little while longer. I want to work around that tree then water both flower beds. I made a crumb cake this morning if you want some." She was

126

so much more home-makerish since she was laid off. In truth Henry did not want her working, and he liked it when she stayed at home. But he did not tell her this. She was a free spirit and thought of herself as unconventional.

"Your doing good with this." He said to her as he admired her gardening ability.

"Finish up soon." He leaned over and gave her another kiss. He hurried into the house and skipped the crumb cake for the moment. He picked up the newspaper and flipped through until he found the classified section. He passed right by the bids section and headed for the pet ads instead. He wanted to get Tabitha a puppy for her birthday. Before coming home he stopped at the Humane Society, but did not find any puppies that Tabitha would like. So he was now looking in the newspaper. He glanced out the front window to see her using the trowel and lining the edge for her flower bed. He sat on the couch and scanned through the ads quickly.

He read through mumbling to himself.

"Border Collie, no. too hyper, Sheepdog, no. too hairy, Whippet, no. too skinny."

He read through each ad finding some imperfection with each breed that was listed. Finally he stopped and smiled.

"English Cocker Spaniel."

He knew that Tabitha loved the movie *Lady and the Tramp* when she was a child. Henry wanted to get Tabitha a beautiful dog that would make a good companion. It had to have a strong sense of confidence yet be affectionate and a good house pet.

"Perfect!" He shouted a bit too loud and sat straight up and dialed the number. He headed into the bedroom with his cell phone just incase Tabitha came in the house; he wanted it to be a surprise.

After he placed the call he was more than pleased with himself. He knew Tabitha would love to get a puppy and the price was very reasonable. The thought it was just what she needed. He went outside to see how she was making out with the planting. Sure enough, she was almost done. She was watering both beds, the final step.

"I'm almost done." She said loudly as he approached her. He whistled again and she smiled. "What do you want to do this afternoon?" He asked her. She picked up her gardening stuff and he assisted her with putting it away in the shed. They headed back to the house.

"I need to get a shower. Then we can go out." She said happily to him. Though money was tighter than it used to be she figured that they would be going out to do something fun. Fun was what she needed.

First they went to go see a movie. Henry preferred action or horror movies, but he knew that she didn't. He took her to see the new Jennifer Anniston movie, Bounty Hunters. He was rather surprised that he liked it. For dinner they went to a Chinese restaurant, which was another good choice that he made. By the end of the night it was still early and they went for a drive. It was almost eight o'clock and they pulled up to an old farm house in the middle of the nowhere. The owner told Henry that they could come anytime before eight-thirty.

"What are we doing here?" She asked as he put the car in park.

"You're present." He replied and smiled. Tabitha was bewildered. They both got of the car and walked up the driveway and to the front of the house. As they neared

Tabitha could hear faint barking and rustling noises coming from just inside the front door. Her curiosity was peaked even more now.

Henry knocked and a minute later an older gentleman appeared at the door.

"Good evening sir. I'm Henry. I called you this afternoon." The older man smiled and invited them in.

"I'm Robert. Nice to meet you." He reached out and shook Henry's hand with surprising strength.

"They're in here if you follow me." Robert was in his mid-fifties and had an English accent. He led the way with Henry and Tabitha following. They crossed the enclosed porch which was larger on the inside than it had looked from the outside.

They stopped at a large fenced in area and Tabitha now saw who was making all of the ruckus. It was puppies.

"Oh my gosh!" Tabitha excitedly gushed and stepped over the fence with Henry.

"Surprise!" He said. "You can have your pick. If you want one." He was hoping that she liked the breed and he could tell from her expression that she did.

"They are little adorable Cocker Spaniels." By now all the puppies were near the two of them nibbling and jumping about.

"I have no idea which one to choose."

Tabitha was beside herself with delight. She picked up and played with each pup.

"Take your time. I'll be back in a minute." Robert was exiting the room.

"Oh honey. This is the best birthday gift ever!" She leaned over and kissed him with one of the pups wrapped up in her arms.

He had done well and was proud of himself. "Do you want a boy or a girl?" he asked.

"I think a girl... it depends on the personality." She already had her choice narrowed down to two girls. One had a more beautiful coat but was kind of shy. The other was not as pretty, but was not timid either and she was very playful.

They both noticed the more playful one and he hoped that would be the one she would choose. It was.

"I love her." Tabitha held and the tiny female pup while it licked her and wagged her small tail.

"She's the one." They both liked the choice. Robert returned and they informed him of the good news. He agreed that each dog has it's own personality and they did good by following their instincts and picking the one that was the best fit for them, not just on appearance. Another fifteen minutes or so had passed and Henry and Tabitha left with their new little puppy.

On the way home they stopped at a pet shop and picked up a few supplies all while escorting their new puppy inside as well. Within that moment all of the worrisome problems that bother Tabitha seemed to evaporate. Now she had a little girl pup and companion to take care of.

Tabitha had decided on the name her Cocker Spaniel Mandy. She had put a lot of care and effort into taking care of Mandy. Tabitha kept very busy with her dog, her garden, and her studies. Henry continued to work and as time went on their financial difficulties lightened. Henry's idea had worked. Tabitha again had goals and plans for the future. They had a greater appreciation for each other and life was good. They had set a date for their beach wedding which would be in late August of the same year. Life was not perfect, but was slowly improving.

In the years that followed, Mandy had changed Tabitha's life for the better. She loved Mandy, and vice versa. They were true companions and Tabitha had felt like a kid again at times. Mandy loved to assist with digging in the garden to help out her owner. Mandy grew into being a very smart and compassionate dog and she made a wonderful pet to Tabitha and Henry's two daughters. Tabitha had finished her writing and English courses and taken a full-time job being a columnist for their local newspaper. She often wrote columns about love, relationships, family, and dogs.

Unit J

Unit J is the Alzheimer's nursing unit at Pleasant Vista Nursing Home. The unit is located at the ground level of the four story building. At any given time there are usually twenty to thirty residents in this unit alone. One of the residents is Jane Hancock. She is seventy-five years young and has had Alzheimer's for the last five years.

Jane has six children, four boys and two girls, all are in their forties and fifties. Her husband had passed away nearly six years ago from severe respiratory problems, COPD and Asthma. She also has ten grandchildren, and five great grand children. Jane's oldest daughter, Lannie, and her husband have power of attorney over Jane's finances and medical care. Like so many families in situations similar it is not uncommon for the adult children to disagree on their elderly parents' medical and legal matters and their general well being. It is most especially true for this family.

Lannie had taken her mother in to live in her home for several years after her father had passed away because Jane needed a lot of extra care. Since Lannie did not work and her husband had quite a bit of money it seemed that Jane's care should be provided by them and in turn gained the power of attorney. The family problems over time regarding Jane's care had continued to multiply and Lannie had to send her mother to live in a nursing home facility. The six siblings all continued to fight; each one of them had their own point of view. None of them were necessarily right or wrong in their opinions, but there was none the less a power struggle between most of Jane's children.

Lannie had put her mother into the first nursing home and she was there for a few months. All of her children visited as often as they could and it was heart breaking to see their mother's mental ability deteriorating over time. None of the children particularly liked the care she was receiving at the home and had brought other suggestions to Lannie's attention for a more suitable situation for their mother.

Jane's younger daughter Danielle was just as devoted to her mother and is equally strong in her opinions about her mother's care. Lannie and Danielle have never gotten along since they were both girls and continued the same way into their adult life. Danielle often visited her mother, several times a week. Jane would not always remember who her children were until after a few minutes of speaking with them and even then she only somewhat remembered. However, there was one family member that she never forgot and loved to talk about when she got company. It was Cassie, their English Springer Spaniel. The family owned her while the kids were going up and into their adolescence. Jane's husband, Doug, had gotten Cassie from a co-worker at the steel mill back in the 1960's. They were giving the pups away and Doug knew it would be a good addition to the family.

Jane loved Cassie's classic English Spaniel look with her white and black coat. She was good with the kids, very playful, and obedient.

Doug made use her assistance with hunting and trained her to be a bird dog. She would often run out ahead and scare up the ruffled grouse and ducks in the brush for Doug to shoot. Cassie was a natural and it was hard to determine whether she liked scaring up the birds the best or retrieving them the best. Doug would often show the old black and white photos of Cassie with her prize in photos at holidays for years to follow. None of Jane's and Doug's children liked to hunt and occasionally Doug and Cassie hunted with the in-laws, but they mostly preferred to go out alone.

All too often Cassie did an excellent job and would they would bring home dinner. Jane was a stay at home mom and would cook whatever Doug and Cassie were able to get. They also had a small farm where they would raise and consume their own chickens, pigs, and turkeys. These are the moments that Jane never forgets.

Christmas season in 2008 Lannie decided to move her mother to Pleasant Vista Nursing Home, which was a very good decision. It was a nice facility, and more centrally located so all Jane's children could get there easier to visit. They had an excellent Alzheimer's care program and better room accommodations. The only negative thing about Lannie's decision is that she did not tell any of her siblings that she moved their mother. Danielle was the first to find out when she went to visit on a Wednesday night, like she always did, thinking that her mother was still at the home. Upon showing up and finding out that her mother was transferred she was understandably upset and beside herself. The nursing staff was not permitted to disclose Jane's new residency. All of the sibilings were shocked that Lannie had acted on that decision and not informed any of them.

Lannie and her family, for the last several years, had no longer celebrated any holiday with any one else in the family. Sam, the youngest brother, and his new wife, Shiela, decided that Christmas Eve to take their mother out of the home so she could visit with her children for Christmas. Lannie had allowed this, it was equally and pleasantly surprised the family when the two of them showed up with Jane. Jane was not in any shape to leave the home as she required a wheelchair most of the time. Sam and Shiela, both being CNA's thought they knew what was best and disregarded the nursing home's instructions. They helped Jane walk and move around; they spent a few hours at Danielle's house with the rest of the family.

It was a joyous night and the family had decided not to gossip about Lannie and her husband, whom were not in attendance. The Hancock's were always a religious family and rejoiced on that Christmas Eve, as they did every year. Despite Jane looking tired, she was in great spirits. Her children and grand children would strike up conversations about the "old days" and Jane would nod and chat along until someone would get on the subject of Cassie. Jane's eyes would widen with excitement and she seemed to lighten up in spirit; it took fifteen years off of her and she was suddenly a younger happier version of herself. The memory of Cassie always had that effect on her.

The grand kids and great grand kids all gathered around and intently listen to Jane tell stories of Cassie and Doug and the rest of the family. All the young kids had seen pictures of Cassie, but did not have the chance to know her. Jane could vividly recall everything, the birds caught, family holidays, digging in the yard, and her playfulness. Anything

and everything that involved Cassie was told and talked
about. Everyone that night was overjoyed and relieved to see
Jane again in her prime. She recalled every detail and fact
and reveled in the moment.

The end of that Christmas evening brought heart full
goodbyes and awakened spirits. Each Hancock, the smallest
to the oldest, felt blessed. Each family left and Sam and
Shield took Jane back to the nursing home. Her memory was
now again failing her, but it wasn't who she really was, there
was so much more to Jane Hancock. Cassie was more than a
beautiful hunting dog; she was their companion, confidant,
and best friend. She completed the Hancock's and left an
undeniable impression on each of them, especially for Jane.
Cassie never realized at the time how over time, she would
be the one common factor who helped keep Jane be herself
and kept the family closely tied.

The Two That Got Away

A lot of dog breeds have a passion and instinct for
hunting and fishing. It is more prevalent in certain breeds. In
the case of the Huntington's coon hound Lucille, it was her
entire being. Thomas and Christy, along with their teenage
son Riley, loved to hunt, camp, and fish. Living out in the
middle of nowhere afforded them to do this as they pleased.
They lived just south of Lake Arthur on route 528.

They often visited the lake to do all of their outdoor
activities. On one particular weekend the family had packed
the bed of their truck with all the necessities and took the
rather short dive to the lake in hopes of getting a prime
location. To them, this was as good as it gets. The spot was
near perfect and for early May the weather was superb.

Lake Arthur, in its shape, resembles a fern leaf. There is a main portion that runs horizontally from east to west with several thinner runs and branches that come off of it. There are two small dams on each end, which Muddy Creek runs through; there are wonderful fishing spots to say the least.

The Huntington's wanted to make a camp on the remnants of an old bridge foundation. The ground was surrounded by large rectangular stones which were a part of the foundation. It used to cross over the large creek before it flooded and was turned into a lake. The spot was large enough for a tent and was surrounded by trees. A beaver dam was adjacent to the area as well as a protected national waterfowl preservation wetland. The hills and mountains were laid out a wonderful landscape against the water.

This spot was located by two other fishing spots and a boat launch, so there were often people who came and went. Off of the main road, route 528, are a few dirt roads which took you to the various scenic and fishing spots. A shut-down dilapidated coal mine lays on the side of the west most mountains which had prompted the state to provide extra clean-up efforts for the area over the last fifty years.

"At least it doesn't take long to get here." Tom remarked to his family as he drove down the dirt no-winter maintenance road to the spot.

He smiled to himself as he loved this area. It was eight o'clock that Friday night and the sunlight being orange and pink as it was gleamed down brightly through the forest and through the truck's windows. Tom had his Ray-Ban's on and glanced at Christy who had her large round gray frames and light purple tinted sunglasses on. They looked like something that Fergie would wear, but Tom thought that they looked better on his wife. Riley bounced around on the

136

backseat. He just turned thirteen the month before and was jamming to his ipod. Next to him was Lucille, their five year old coonhound. She panted and sniffed out the top of the window, which was down a pinch for her. Lucille loved the woods just as much as her owners. Car rides for Lucille almost always meant being outdoors.

The navy blue Ford pickup neared the spot and pulled off in the side dirt parking area to see if any one was at the spot.

"Oh good, it's not taken." Christy said. They all breathed the same happy sigh of relief. Even though they lived a five or so minutes from there they hoped it would be unoccupied so they wouldn't have to wait or come back. Tom turned the truck around and backed down the hill towards the water. A minute later they were there, unpacking would only take a minute or two and they would be off to their comfort zones.

Tom was out of the truck first. There were only two boats out on the lake and he admired how the light from the sunset shown and glistened across the surface of the water. Christy had noticed the beauty of it also and never got tired of it. To her it looked like thousands of crystals dancing on the water. Riley was less interested in looking at the water and more interested in taking Lucille for a walk and letting her swim for a bit.

Lucille was out of the truck. She panted from the heat and went directly to the water's edge to get a drink. Riley followed her; holding her extension leash. Lucille was not a prissy dog by any means. She loved water, anything to get dirty. Though there are a couple types of coonhounds, Lucille was Black and Tan Coonhound. Her coat was just that, black and tan. The Huntington's had gotten her from a breeder when she was eight weeks old. She was the runt of

137

the litter and had cost very little. The family did not care that she was a tad smaller for her size. They loved her fearless attitude the most. The family wanted first most to get a dog that would be intelligent and a good family pet. Since they avidly loved hunting and fishing a Coonhound seemed to fit most appropriately.

Tom and Christy had continued to unload the truck while Riley and Lucille explored. "Come on over here." Riley had said to Lucy, he often called her Lucy so the dog's name didn't sound too formal. Lucy and Riley jogged on the shore and Lucy decided to go traipsing through the new growth of cattails.

"Just watch out for the turtles and beavers!" Christy yelled over to Riley.

"Ok mom!" loudly replied back. Setting up the camp only took five minutes. They didn't bring much and if they needed anything else one of them would just run home and come back.

The family had planned on going night fishing. The catfish in this lake were legendary. More than once a state record size have been pulled out of there and Tom knew that the big catfish came out at night. Each of them had their favorite type of bait. Tom used beef liver, the bloodier the better he always said. Christy preferred salmon eggs, and Riley went with the traditional night crawler.

"No baby one-footer's tonight!" Tom said enthusiastically and took a *high-five* position.

"Yeah!" Riley approved and completed the high-five. The camp site was complete, hooks baited, and dusk had fallen.

Another truck had pulled into the other spot and two older men were fishing there. They did not have any camping gear and would not be there all night.

"Riley, get those logs from over there so I can get the fire started." Christy stayed sitting in the camping chair with Lucy next to her while Tom and Riley gathered up firewood.

"Whoo hoo!" Exclaimed one of the men who appeared to have caught some type of perch or crappie. "I can't wait till we get one dad." Riley was excited and loved spending time fishing.

It was nearly nine thirty and they had caught a few catfish, but nothing "major" as Riley liked to put it. They munched on chips and drank sodas while waiting for the big one. Often with their fishing history they always caught the really big ones after eleven. One of the older fisherman had came over to say hi and to see what the Huntington's had caught. This did not bother Tom one bit. He loved to chat about fishing. Lucy had barked a little, but her leash was tied to a tree and she was sitting close to Christy.

"Haven't got much yet. A few small ones and a lot of bites." Tom had said to the fisherman. He in return had said that he and his brother had got a crappie and a small bass. They wished each other luck and the fisherman had returned to his spot.

Lucy was now near Tom she was being mostly being on guard as the proud protector of the Huntington's, but she abandoned her post for a few minutes to snuggle by Tom. He was her favorite person and though she loved each family member there was no doubt that Tom was her master. He patted her head and back and kept an eye on his bobber. It was vibrating ever so often and he waited for the moment to pull back. Lucy retired on a sleeping bag and Tom watched his pole with intensity. The yellow fluorescent bobber hit the pole and Tom wasted no time. He jumped up instinctively and yanked up and back with his fishing pole.

The bobber was off laying somewhere on the ground and he was reeling in the line with great difficulty. The excitement not only had caught their attention, but also the attention of the other two fishermen. Christy had gotten a pair of thick rubber gloves and the net in anticipation while Riley cheered his dad on. All Lucy could do is bark. The line was tight and moving from side to side as the fish attached tried to break free. The fiberglass pole could be heard crackling and Tom had prayed that it would not break.The two fishermen came over to see if they could offer assistance and were particularly curious about what kind of fish was on the line.

"It's big! Really big! I'm having a heck of a time." Tom nearly had the fish out to the shore and surfaced at the top of the water.

"Oh my God!" Tom exclaimed and could not believe his eyes. One of the fishermen let out a profanity of some sort and the group assisted the best they could.

"That's a Muskie! Has to be at least five foot!" yelled the other man. Christy held out the net and was shocked by the size of the fish.

"That's the biggest fish I've ever seen that wasn't in an aquarium!" She was shocked. Riley was stunned as well and Lucy barked even more furiously now at the sight of the monster fish.

Tom tried to get the fish into the net, which probably wouldn't have held the fish very effectively due to its sheer size; it did not work. Tom's pole itself looked like a fish hook being so bent. The pole finally snapped and the fish bit the line and escaped.

"Awe." Was the unanimous response among the crowd. Lucille's barking had diminished and sat next to Tom looking up at him.

"It got away girl." He petted her head and her tail thumped away leaving a small cloud of dust.

"I can't believe how big that was!" The group was in shock and enthralled by the experience.

"Oh, I should have gotten a picture of it. It all happened so fast." Cindy was disappointed as the whole experience did happen so fast none of them could almost believe it.

"Thanks guys for coming over to help." Tom said.

"No problem. I'm Gus and this is my brother Marley." Handshakes were exchanged and the stories started. The two brothers stayed at the Huntington's site for a bit and they all fished, sat by the fire, and shared tales. Lucille had warmed up to them as well. She had stopped barking and got comfy sitting with them. She was a good judge of character and could tell that these were good people.

"That one could have been a record for this lake." Gus had said and Tom listened with interest as he relined and salvaged what was left of his pole. The next half hour didn't bring to many bites, just a lot of good times shared. The night air was getting colder and Christy had bundled up in a hoodie and with blanket wrapped around her. She had taken her pole out of the water and just sat near the fire and relaxed with Lucy. Tom and Riley were as wide-eyed as ever. They had a good feeling that they would get another huge fish before retiring for the night. They were right.

The second whopper of a fish was caught about forty-five minutes after the first one was caught. Awe had struck the group again. Tom had put a different bobber on his pole this time. It was a plastic yellow and orange one. Lucy went crazy barking as she saw the bobber fly up and hit the pole with so much force that it shattered.

"Oh!" Riley said as Tom grabbed is pole and yanked again. "Here we go again!" Tom yelled as the line pulled vigorously. If he hadn't been standing right there he would have lost the pole in the water for sure.

The line went slack and Tom thought for sure that the fish had snapped or bitten the line. Yet in truth, the monstrous fish was swimming towards the shore. Tom kept reeling in and kept an eye on the line. He wasn't totally convinced that the fish was off the hook. Gus, Marley, and Riley were all standing next to Tom when he reeled the fish closer to shore and began to bring it in. Christy and Lucy sat this one out; they left it to the men since they were in there element.

Bubbles came to the top of the surface and with one more forceful yank the fish's head appeared just out of the water.

"Holy crap!" exclaimed Tom. It was a catfish, and not just any catfish. If none of them had seen it with their own eyes they would not have believed it. The head of the catfish was at least three feet wide. Its tail was near the surface and made large waves and a whoosh sound as it moved back and forth. What was left of Tom's fishing pole cracked continuously and Tom feared the worse. It was not as feisty as the Muskie, yet was easily three times the size. The awe, shock, and excitement had hit all of them again. Christy quickly got up and raced for the camera. Though it was dark she was sure she could get a half-way decent picture of it. Lucy bent ballistic and her coon dog instincts took over. She growled, barked, and paced continuously at the monster with whiskers. It must have looked like a huge cat to her with having large whiskers like that.

The catfish was now more alert due to the entire ruckus from the barking and people yelling. Now the fish seemed determine to get free. It didn't take much. A few tugs were all it took. It literally pulled Tom to the ground, yet he kept grip of the pole. A loud "snap" was heard and that was it. The catfish had snapped the line, broke the remained of the fishing pole, and took off. Tom sat there in the dirt on the shore looking at his pole. Riley had helped his dad off of the ground and all were in a frenzy about the near record catfish, again. Christy had almost made it to take the picture, but didn't get it. By the time she got the camera, turned it on, readjusted the settings to night mode, and got close enough it was gone and her husband was sitting in the dirt.

"Darn!" Christy exclaimed with the camera in hand. She touched Tom's shoulder that was still shaking from all the excitement.

"I'm so sorry honey that it got away. We may need stronger poles and line." She had said to him. Tom took it all in stride.

"How would be have gotten it home?" Riley said.

"I can't believe how big it was!" Gus and Marley had joined in once again and were grateful for the exciting night and the new people that they just met. Lucy had enough for one night and went off to lie in the tent. The Huntington's had started to put some of the fishing gear away and Gus and Marley had said their goodbyes and made their way to their truck.

It was nearly midnight and all were tired. Tom had stoked the fire and turned on a portable heater in the tent. Riley laid down next to Lucy and zippered himself up. Tom and Christy sat outside for a few minutes more and admired the stars and the moonlight reflecting on the water.

"It's beautiful out, but a little cold." Christy said sitting next to Tom.

"Yes it is." He replied. She put her head on his shoulder and yawned.

"I can't believe those two got away." He said to her. They retired to the tent, dreamt of fish, and looked forward to the following day.

The Long Awaited Deliverance

John and Dottie owned a ranch in Utah just on the outskirts of Salt Lake City. The property was located at the base of a mountain; it held their home and their farm. In addition to John and Dottie were their four children, all of which were John's from his first marriage, and Maxine, their seven-year old Australian Shepherd mix.

Maxine was more than just the family's dog; she was the farm's dog also. Sheriff of the barnyard and top dog on the range, at least that's what the family had joked about. She took her herding very seriously after a long lineage of herding and seven years being on the job she never let any of them down. There were horses, pigs, sheep, goats, chickens, and one impossibly rogue turkey.

John's profession by day Monday through Friday is a CPA. Being a partner in an accounting company in Salt Lake brought long hours that extended beyond five pm. Dottie understood and never complained. They were married for several years and life to them was as good as it could be.

John was not like the average business partner. He never took his work home and he never worried about work until he begun his daily commute. He was a man whom for part of the week wore a suit and the other majority of the time wore coveralls. The contrast was welcomed only because the later was who he really was.

Dottie worked as well; she was CEO of the house, a traditional grand-style farm house, and also of the farm. The kids all helped and did their usual chores, but the most valuable of all the farm hands was the one who lacked hands, Maxine. She was the faithful farm assistant and Dottie's best friend.

Being a young age of twenty-four Dottie had a lot of responsibilities. She loved the roominess of their home and life in the country. Growing up was difficult for Dottie and her two brothers. She was the middle child and grew up with her mother and step-father in Salt Lake City. The family had lived in low-income government housing. She liked the clean air, mountain views, and abundance of stars that filled the night sky. Often at night after the kids were all in bed her and Maxine would sit on the porch and gaze dreamily up at the sky. She'd picture what lay beyond the stars and her thoughts filled her heart with comfort.

The sun rose early most mornings which gave rise to the family and all the farm animals. Maxine was the self-appointed sheriff of the farm. I guess being a Sheppard gave her the right. She was up early every morning getting the animals up and feeding them; the roosters also assisted in this process. The five-thirty a.m. patrol began. For two hours she walked like a mall cop would, around the perimeter over and over. She made nodding gestures or glared suspiciously, depending on which ever the moment called for.

Maxine often had to wrangle that previously mentioned trouble-making turkey. He was a pure white albino turkey, Whitey. He often escaped from his pen and tried eloping from the barnyard whenever it was convenient, or not convenient. Whitey answered to no one and he gave Maxine a run for her money.

"Mom! Whitey's out again!" Mike, the youngest son yelled. Dottie walked out the back screen door and down the porch steps to catch a glance.

"That darn turkey is going to get it. We may have to eat him one of these years." She commented to herself shaking her head and drying her hands on the dish towel and headed towards the barn in disgust.

"Maxine!" Dottie bellowed. Around the corner came Maxine. She was not walking, but not at a full sprint either. She had a cocky attitude about her like a bouncer that knows he's going to have to throw someone out of the club. It was unpleasant, dutiful, and annoying for Maxine to take care of Whitey.

She was now following the scent of the turkey. He was not too far ahead and Maxine was determined to catch up quickly. She lost the bouncer attitude and was now running on an irate postal worker mentality. She had so much going on. She had just finished rounding up the chickens that were dispersedly wandering away from the barn and now she had to deal with that darn turkey again.

"Good dog." Dottie commented and stood there with Mike and John watching Maxine follow the scent and do what she was bred to do, round up risque' turkeys. Dottie and John were pleased with how well Maxine did her job. "I'll go and get him." John said.

146

Maxine had Whitey in her sights and slowly approached from behind. John was just starting to walk in the direction that Maxine took off to. Whitey was not as pretty as other turkeys, being born albino was the main reason. His feathers were pure white, but always looked tinged and matted. It looked like someone tried to pluck him, but missed. His beard and beak were a faded red in color. His personality had matched his looks, piss and vinegar. Whitey was constantly caperous and was one ticked-off turkey.

Maxine didn't care about the way he looked or his demeanor. She only cared when he stayed in his pen and brought it to John and Dottie's attention when he was elusive. Whitey had almost made it to the border of the property of the fifty-five acres when Maxine had caught up to him. She snuck up, darted, and cut him off. In protest the turkey turned up the attitude full blast and gobbled furiously at his keeper, his nemesis, that diligent herding dog.

John was jogging now as he'd seen the pair up ahead of him.

"Good girl." He praised her. John had the twine lead ready and didn't have much difficulty looping it over Whitey's head. It took a moment, but the turkey stood perfectly still except for his bobble head which was making a rubber-necking motion.

"Got it!" He was happy with himself and acknowledged Maxine's stealth in subduing Whitey's latest escape plan.

"You are a persistent pain in my butt." He led the turkey back to the barn with Maxine following behind like a warden. The three of them headed back. The morning began with an adventurous start.

After the turkey was secured, at least for the time being, John walked in the house and headed straight for the kitchen sink. He poured out a generous amount of liquid soap and washed his hands. Dottie was making vegetable soup in the crock pot and looked up at him and sighed.

"You feeling any better hun?" He asked her with concern and care in his choice of words. "Only threw up once today. It's an improvement." She sat down at the kitchen table looking up at John and smiled through her exhausted outward appearance. He returned the smile and sat next to her. His hand wiped a large bead of sweat off his forehead. She looked so tired and he was empathizing with her the best he could.

"Soooo." He started to say, and curtsied around the subject, but finally asked. "Should we start thinking of names?" Her eyes widened and she stood up and was now flustered. The tiredness was gone. That was what he was afraid of when he spoke.

"No. we shouldn't. I don't want to jinx it." She said demandingly to him.

"It's not a jinx. It's been four months. I think we are safe." He sheepishly replied.

He continued since she didn't immediately fire back at him. "The doctor says it's safer once three months has passed. Now we're almost done with the forth month." Dottie bit her bottom lip and another small sigh crept out. She said nothing, just continued to stir the crock pot. "I know." Was all she could manage to say at first then she heavy-heartedly continued. "We've already lost two.... I couldn't stand it to happen again." John understood and dropped the subject. It was a sensitive topic for both of them.

Maxine came in through her doggy door and started wagging her tail. "Here girl. You did a good job this morning, huh?" Dottie poured Maxine a full bowl of cold water and finished cleaning the kitchen before their late morning walk, which the two of them took everyday.

They walked from one corner to the other, then back. It was a few miles, but they took it slower lately. Dottie always brought along her cell phone and bottle of water, just in case. The rest of the family was gone for the day. John had to run to the office on an emergency so he dropped off the two younger kids at his parent's house on the other side of the town and the older two kids were headed out to a birthday party and sleepover.

There was nothing that Dottie appreciated more than her family, their home, and the dog, with the exception of some quiet time once in a while. Maxine and Dottie continued to walk, both were striding and both were silent. Taking in the crisp air and sunshine Dottie felt grateful and knew she was wrong for snapping at John. She decided to surprise John by picking up a Baby Name Book later in town that day.

A long five months had passed and Dottie was still taking her walks. Her and Maxine went slower and took longer, but the exercise was good and necessary. For a December afternoon the weather was remarkable. There were only a few inches of snow with mild temperatures. Her brown furry boots weren't really needed but carried her to the stables and back to the house. It was a short ten minute walk, but that was all she needed.

It was the same walk basically, on the ranch with Maxine by her side. The only real difference besides the weather was her belly. She was thirty-nine weeks along and ready to pop. It had been a long and difficult pregnancy. There was sickness, ER visits, appointments twice a week, and lots of worry. The end was almost near with one week to go. She and John had finally decided on names. Josie for a girl and Robert for a boy, they wanted to be surprised at the time of delivery which was rare now and days. Being so close to the delivery time she was finally starting to relax. The memories of her two previous miscarriages were just that, memories. John, her, and the kids had the present and their newest family member due to arrive – soon.

Of course, the one invaluable member of the family was there right beside her still, as always, Maxine. She was the one who gave her courage and hope and had helped Dottie get through the longest nine months of her life. Whitey, however didn't make it. He got loose a few months back and it was his last wander over near the stable. Their palomino didn't like the turkey snooping and one swift kick from the palomino did him in, quickly.

This would be Dottie's last walk for a while. She and Maxine got back to the house and she had a sharp piercing abdomen pain. This was it; the long awaited deliverance was here. Ten hard hours later in the same hospital that she was born in Dottie gave birth to a blonde-haired baby girl, Josie. She weighed six pounds and seven ounces, the same birth weight as her mother and coincidently at the same time seven o' four pm.

Dottie, John, the kids, and Maxine all welcomed home the newest member of the family three days later.

Quite the Pair

Kathy is a successful business owner in her early forties. She had a son, Josh, and a daughter, Jamie. Her children were fraternal twins, both being eight years old, and both wanting a pet of their own. Kathy was a recent divorcee and thought a pet for both of them would be beneficial.

Kathy, whom owned a small book store in Buffalo, lived on the outskirts of the city and the three of them resided in Orchard Park. It was a small community, well-kept and quite except for football season being that it was also home to the Buffalo Bills. Kathy and her two children were quite the sports fans. Josh and Jamie decided that no matter what pets they picked they would name them after their favorite players.

"Red and blue all the way!" Josh would often yell when he got excited about the Bills.

Josh wanted a dog. He played half-back for the local youth football team, The Bisons. Jamie also was athletic and took part in gymnastics. Her gymnastic outfit was red and blue as were the Bison's jerseys. Their father had left and abandoned all of them and moved to the other side of the country, Seattle. It was a hard few months with lots of adjustments but the three of them did the best they could and prevailed.

Now that the children were getting older the idea of owning a pet opened new thoughts to Kathy as it meant companionship, responsibility, and a watchdog. She knew that Josh wanted a dog and Jamie wanted a cat. Co-habitation would be an issue, but her plan was that she wanted get a young puppy and a young kitten in hopes they would get along if raised together. Kathy had been busy doing research as to what breeds they would adopt.

The kittens were the easier choice of the two. Jamie loved Siamese cats and they were relatively easy to find. Most kittens are "Free to Good Homes" which really means that the owners are happy with anyone who takes them so there isn't a box of young kittens living on their front porch. The dog, on the other hand, is a harder choice which requires more thought and consideration. Josh wanted a large dog; he often talked about Mastiffs and Labs which was suiting for them since Kathy would feel safer with a large dog in the house.

The upcoming Saturday the family arranged to meet with an elderly woman who was giving away Siamese kittens. The three of them piled up in the Durango after Jamie's gymnastic lesson and were on their way.

"Mom, I hope the kittens are pretty and perfect." Kathy smiled and replied.

"I'm sure you will find the right one." Josh yawned a lot in boredom and had no concern for cats, he wanted a dog. Jamie was excited to no end and after a twenty minute drive they arrived at the old Victorian home on the west side of Buffalo.

It was summertime and an elderly lady was sitting in a white wicker glider on her front porch when the family pulled up. They all walked towards the house, Jamie had the largest grin on her face that he mother had ever seen.

"Hi there. I'm Kathy and this is Jamie and Josh, my two children. I called a few days ago about the kittens."

"Oh yes. Hello. I'm Laurie. Come on up and take a look." The two kids ran up first and saw the older woman gesture to the cardboard box to the left side of the porch.

"Aww!" Jamie exclaimed. She thought they were all so cute and pretty. Both kids picked up several of the kittens and held them. Josh's expression of boredom had soon passed and he was almost as excited as Jamie.

The box contained male and female kittens. Some had longer hair and some with shorter hair.

"Blue, brown, or green eyes?" Jamie had asked herself as she took in each kitten. Each one was unique and beautiful, for Jamie it was a difficult choice. Finally, one was chosen it was a long-haired female with green eyes.

"She's perfect. Mom, can I have this one?" Jamie asked with a smiled and held up the kitten in front of her. Kathy knelt down and held the kitten for a minute.

"She's great." Kathy said. "But you need to ask the lady."

Jamie went up to Laurie and politely asked. Of course Laurie had said.

"Yes." And she was very pleased to see that the children had manners, to her it was refreshing. Jamie was so excited she had thanked the woman and gave her a hug. Kathy carefully placed the small kitten in the travel carrier and secured it in the back of their navy blue Durango.

"Do you think she is ok back there?" Jamie was concerned about her new kitten.

"She's fine Jamie. The crate is secured tightly and she has that small blanket in there too." Jamie was happy and now was busily thinking of names. Even though her and her brother discussed that they were going to name their pets after their favorite players it just didn't seem suitable now. Jamie pondered for a bit and out of nowhere exclaimed the kitten's name.

"Jasmine! Mom, what do you think?" Kathy loved it but chose her words carefully to her daughter.

"Jamie it is completely up to you. This is your cat and will be for a long time. Since she is yours and your responsibility you can chose whatever name you think is fitting for her." Jamie was sure and said.

"Jasmine it is." They were close to arriving home and Josh was antsy even more about getting a dog. He knew it would happen soon and he tried to be patient the best he could.

"Mom when do I get a puppy?" Josh pleadingly asked.

"Very soon. I have to call around to some breeders and keep answering ads. Dogs are harder sometimes to find the right one." He looked slightly disappointed, but kept his head up.

"Ok. Mom." He knew not to rush or be whinny, and then it would take longer to get a dog.

All Josh thought about that week following Jamie getting her kitten was dogs, dogs, and dogs. In between working and family time Kathy searched several ads looking for the right dog. She knew the selection was all about breed, size, and temperament. Finally, she found an ad on Craigslist for Bernese Mountain Dog puppies. They were seven weeks old and ready to leave the following week. She called the owner who lived in the city of Buffalo and had gotten a lot of information on the pups. There were still two males and two females left that have not been selected yet. The kids and she were going to look at the puppies tomorrow.

Bernese Mountain dogs, characteristically, are a large breed, good with children and other pets, and make excellent watchdogs. She liked what she heard from the owner and the long list of doggy specifics that she was looking for was now a list full of *yes* for each item. Though it was not a breed of dog that Josh had thought about, or even heard about, his mother had bought a book from her store and showed it to Josh and explained about these types of dogs. Josh liked what he saw; he liked the dark colored fur and the large size of the adults was more than willing to go see the puppies.

"Do you think the dog will fit in?" Josh asked his mother.

"I hope so. We can go tomorrow and take a look at the puppies. As far as what I've seen and heard they are a good match, but the only way to know for sure is to see them and what they are like." She reassured him and added. "If these puppies aren't the right match then we can keep looking, but I think it is worth a shot." Josh smiled and anticipated going to see the puppies in the morning.

Before they went to go see the puppies they stopped at a pet supply store just a few blocks from where Kathy's store was located. They knew they were getting a puppy soon, but they also knew it wouldn't be today. If they liked the Bernese Mountain dog pups they would select and reserve today and could bring one home in a week. They selected a large bag of puppy food, matching water and food bowls, a medium-sized dog bed, leash, crate, collar, etcetera. The rear of the Durango was full. All three of them liked the picking out the dog supplies, especially Josh. Now the feeling that he was really going to get a puppy was settling in. Even Jamie like looking at the dog supplies and was pleased that her kitten was doing well. Jasmine, thankfully, was easy going and Kathy was hopeful that bringing in an additional family member would work out and be unanimous for all. After leaving the pet store and headed for the breeder's home.

The mountainous towering house seemed perfect for the mountainous sized canines that resolved there. Despite Kathy's preconceived ideas about the owners she was surprised to meet the owner and to see that she was in her mid-thirties and petite with black hair, yet she had sounded older on the phone. It looked as if one of these canines could easily knock her down with a single whack of one of their tails.

"Hi." The polite and petite woman said as she walked out to the gate to let the family in.

"You must be Kathy."

"I am and these are my children Josh and Jamie."

"I'm Marcy." The black-haired petite woman extended and shook Kathy's hand and all walked towards the house.

Two of the adult dogs were walking around the yard and did bark, but were secured on running leashes. "Don't mind them. The puppies are on the side in the enclosed porch." Marcy said and pointed to the south side of her house. The enclosed porch had black siding and looked very much different from the red brick main portion of the historic-looking house. They walked up to the white aluminum screen door; Marcy opened it and they all went inside.

Half of the enclosed porch was sectioned off into an area for the puppies. They were one week away from going to their new homes for the lucky ones who were reserved. Marcy said to the group.

"The ones with the blue and pink collars are still available. Blue for boy and pink for girl. The white and black collared ones have already been selected. It helps keep them straight. Go ahead and look if you want." The kids were wide-eyed and could not wait to play with the puppies. She didn't have to tell them twice. Their mom gave them the ok and off they went.

Surveying, picking-up, holding, and tossing toys and balls. Just about anything they could do with the puppies they did. Though Jamie loved Jasmine she took the opportunity to join and have fun. Jamie immediately had her favorite, a girl with blue eyes, but she had kept her opinion to herself as this was Josh's dog and he got to choose.

"Hey boy! Fetch!" Josh tossed a purple rubber ball to the other side of the enclosure and the small male pup went after it while most of the other dogs were more interested in chewing their toys or playing with Jamie.

Josh had taken to this dog right away and this pup was giving him all the attention in the world in return. All of the puppies seemed intelligent and were friendly, but Josh knew right away this was the dog he wanted.

"So what do you think champ?" Kathy had asked Josh after being there for almost half an hour.

"He's the one." Josh said as he kept playing with the puppy. Kathy knew that was the one he was going to choose.

"It's official then!" Marcy was just as happy as the family was. Kathy paid her deposit for the dog and arranged to pick it up the following Saturday, a week later.

It was difficult for Josh to leave his new pup and had to spend another week being dogless. The thought was calming and comforting to him that would be able to bring his dog home very soon.

That week flew by for Kathy. Her store never seemed so busy and she worked later every night. When the kids were done with school every day were dropped off at their grandparent's house until she was done working. All Josh did was talk about the puppy and played football in the yard. He decided the name Jim was perfect, after Jim Kelly.

"Jim loves to play ball just like me." He told his grandfather as he threw a pass which whizzed by his grandfather.

"That's great Josh. Hey you got quite the arm." Josh jogged and retrieved the football. It was signed by Jim Kelley and it was Josh's favorite thing in the world – next to his new puppy.

By Friday night the dog's area was all set up and they had every necessary supply imaginable. Jasmine had a vet appointment that week and she was administered her shots and was given a clean bill of health. Jim was not even at his new home yet, but had a vet appointment scheduled for the following week. They were more than prepared. Josh could barely get to sleep that night and Saturday slowly came.

They were meeting the owner, Marcy, at ten that morning. Josh had his Bisons jersey on and was ready. Jamie slept over a friend's house and did not need to be picked up until gymnastics was over that afternoon. It was just Kathy and Josh who finished getting ready in a hurry and left. Kathy had reminded him.

"Now, since this is the first day that all the puppies can leave there may be other people picking up their dogs. If there are then we may need to wait our turn. So please try to be patient." They arrived at the monstrous home again and this time the gate was open and there were five other vehicles there. A plethora of excited families and even more excited children were all over Marcy's yard and inside the enclosed porch.

"Hi." Kathy said to Marcy as they approached the house.

"Lots of people here today."

"Yep." Marcy replied, but she was scattered-brained from all of the families talking and all the preparation to send the puppies to their new homes.

"Go ahead in and find your puppy. Did you pick out a name for him Josh?" Josh smiled and replied.

"Yes. I did. It's Jim, after Jim Smith."

"Nice name." Marcy replied. She was impressed and an avid Bills fan herself and the fact that most kids picked the typical doggy names, Fido and such.

Josh recognized Jim the moment he saw him.

"Here boy!" Josh called out and the puppy came right over wagging his tail intently and Josh picked him up. Soon after they finished chatting with Marcy and the other owners and before they knew it they were on their way home with Jim secured in the back of the vehicle. "I think he likes his name." Josh told his mom. She was confident in the selection of the dog and was glad that her son did not pick a ridiculous name for him.

In the days following Jim had adjusted to his new home and owners well. He also liked the cat, but Kathy had thought to herself. "Who wouldn't love her with that adorable face?" Jasmine was just as equally fond of Jim. For a puppy he towered over the black and brown fuzz ball yet she found comfort being in his presence. They romped and played together as two other pets would and at night they slept near each other cuddled up in the same pet bed. Even though Jim was Josh's dog and Jasmine was Jamie's cat the two pets seemed to belong to each other more than to their people.

Josh and Jamie continued to do excellent in school, sports, and at home. They had overcome the hardship that occurred to them over the last few months. Life continued and life was good. The three of them, and the two pets, had a lot to look forward to and happiness was shared. Kathy was quite pleased with herself and her children's choices in pets and she was quite proud of them. As for Jim, the Bernese Mountain dog, and Jasmine, the Siamese cat, they enjoyed each other's company and put the saying *fighting like cats and dogs* to shame, they were quite the pair.

For Laughs

Dog on the Run

Jason and I were driving into the city of Butler to do some shopping on a sunny spring afternoon. While driving east down New Castle Hill road we spotted a rather disturbing sight. A light-colored medium sized dog was running down the hill. Periodically, he was darting in and out of the traffic and he looked scared and lost to say the least. He ran around, stopping and then starting again. Several cars honked, but continued driving. No one was going to do a thing except for us.

As we neared the dog it looked like a Shar Pei. He was tan with a black nose and eyes and of course all the wrinkly skin; the breed was unmistakable. Fortunately I spotted that he had a dark blue collar on with tags. We wanted to stop and try to catch him so we could locate the owner. We were fearful that one of the cars would hit him next time he leapt into the traffic.

Jason had a wildly-excited look in his eye. He was definitely an adrenaline junky most of the time and him jumping from a moving vehicle was right up his alley.

"Put on your flashers and slow down." I had done so, now fearing that Jason would get hurt as would the dog.

"The poor thing is going to get hit!" I nervously exclaimed as speed racer dog decided to run into the street again. Two cars swerved and laid on their horns. We were past the Shar Pei now.

"I'm going to turn around up ahead and we can try it again." Jason agreed with me and he nodded his head. He was not taking his eyes off the dog.

I pulled into the parking lot of a run-down looking mechanic shop and turned around. Driving now I was headed up the large hill instead of down. The dog had temporarily stopped and seemed confused. He was at least back on the same side of the road that we were on. Luckily there were no cars behind us for a while. I drove slow, putting the flashers on again and approached the dog. I eased up the hill and Jason prepared himself to jump out and grab him.

We almost reached the dog and he began to run again. He stayed curbside and was running towards us down the hill.

"This is not a good idea." I said doubting our plan.

"Stop.....now!" Jason yelled.

I stopped and he jumped out. He instantly knelt on the ground next to the car with his arms out hoping to grab the dog. The Shar Pei, aka speed racer, did not stop nor did he slow down or even notice Jason; he ran past him like Jason was not even there. Jason lunged, but missed and his upper body now landed halfway out on the ground.

I looked up and saw some cars were starting up the hill behind me. "Crap."

"Get in!" I yelled. Jason did just that and I continued up to the top of the hill. He slid his seatbelt back on and looked out the side mirror and I glanced up in the rearview mirror. The dog made one more mad dash into traffic and luckily made it back out and went up a side road. "His luck is going to run out soon." Jason said.

"At least he's up on the side street now and not in the main traffic." I replied.

"He was running fast! Must have had tunnel vision, bad. He didn't even make eye contact with me." Jason was breathing normal now and had recuperated from the rescue attempt.

"At least we tried. No one else did. I hope he makes it home safe." I was somewhat relieved that he was no longer on the main road. We both hoped that his owner found him and we had continued on our way.

We wanted to return him to his owner, but that did not happen. The Shar Pei was gone. A mad rushing scared dog running in and out of traffic only spells disaster. Like any animal near a road the results can be devastating. This dog, on this afternoon was beyond lucky and Jason and I hope that the speed-racing Shar Pei had retired from his kamikaze antics and made it safely home.

Sidecar Sidekicks

A picture is worth a thousand words. I believe that is how the saying goes. One dog picture in particular caught my attention. It was a fabulous black and white photo in the book *Mondo Canine*, page 76. The contents in this picture show a biker, perhaps not the smelly bad-ass type of biker, but none the less it was a man wearing leather sitting on his motorcycle. He wore a pair of dark sunglasses, a white helmet, and had an odd expression. Even with intently studying the photo I cannot determine if the man was holding back a smile or perhaps was trying to look too serious. One can only speculate without talking to the man himself.

The scene in the picture was on a roadway. The rear of the car in front of the cycle was dark in color and only the back corner was visible. The motorcycle sat behind the first car, amidst in the middle of two cars. The car directly behind the motorcycle was also dark colored, an SS Charger. Definitely an antique by today's standard, but was the cat's meow at the time – or rather would it be the dog's bark at the time?

I'm sure the passenger whom was accompanying the motorcycle man in the picture would agree with the later. Yes, the dog's bark fits nicely for this pic. The passenger was a black lab standing in the motorcycle's sidecar. The adult dog wearing the white sunglasses and matching white helmet is the unusual and humorous part of the picture. This dog seems quite content standing there as his masters side. He looks like a real biker, this dog, and is more bad-ass-ish than his owner. He is firm and stands tall in the sidecar, just being there and being free. No hidden smile behind biker's goggles, just a free spirit wanting to be on the road.

Perhaps the human and canine pair are riding to the coast? From the east coast to the west coast, that's what freedom in America is about. Master and dog, they have each other, their freedom to ride, and their motorcycle with sidecar. "Did this commandeering pooch really rule and ride the road?" I still wonder as I look at the photograph. When it comes to freedom, I hope so. When it comes to safety, I hope not.

The canine helmet is a nice and necessary touch, but the appearance of an unsuspected pothole or absent-minded driver could send the unrestrained dog flying through the air and fighting for his life.

"Did they ever really shoot dogs out of cannons?" They better not have and I would hate to see this free-riding pooch parish from his owner's preferred method of transportation. The price of freedom is in one's own mind and perception.

One weekend while visiting with my family at the cabin I had an interesting experience in observing another free-riding pooch or perhaps he wasn't so free-willed and instead it was the actions of an ignorant SOB.

This was also a black lab. He had a high-rise prime riding position in the back of his owner's pickup truck. Not only did this pooch get to ride in the rear of the truck, he also had his own large platform that he got to ride on top of. It was an over-sided large utility box that sat squarely in the rear of the truck and took up the entire bed. The dog sat atop of the faux steel pedestal of doom. The black lab had a leash tied to the antenna of the pickup, but there was no railing or any type of safety feature. *What the heck!* The dog itself was higher than the roof of the cab. I wonder what the clearance of the pickup now is.

My jaw dropped at least two inches when I saw the abomination. My mother was in the passenger seat and Amber sat in the backseat. The truck with the dare-devil canine pulled out in front of us on Route 6 and was headed east.

"Look at that idiot!" My mother exclaimed and Amber followed her comment with a "Wow!" I was speechless for a minute. I wanted to follow the truck and give the driver a piece of my mind at the right opportunity, but fear of road rage kept my anger at bay.

I was furious, but kept my driving steady. At least the speed limit was only thirty-five mph and I kept my car at a reasonable distance behind the truck, just in case. I was only behind the pickup for a mile or so, by then the truck continued forward down Route 6 and I turned into the parking lot of the only grocery store in Smethport. My mother wrote down the plate and vehicle information and I called the police. The state police barracks were only two miles down the road and I prayed for the dog's sake that a trooper would respond before the speed limit increased to fifty-five.

"I can't believe this guy!" I yelled when the pickup sped up and kept driving. I yelled some sort of profanity out the window to the redneck beer-gut wannabe, but he never heard me. His muffler was too loud and was nearly off as it was dragging from behind the pickup.

All I could do is report the driver and hoped something would be done about it. In the past while traveling on the interstate I've had to make a few calls to the state police about reckless drivers. I had one semi for a major soda company whom continually swerved in and out of two lanes of traffic. He nearly hit at least ten cars, that I counted, and went off of the road several times. Well, I followed the truck for fifteen miles, as we were both headed north. I kept my distance and in that space of time not one Pennsylvania trooper responded. Nice to know our tax dollars are hard at work.

If the state police responded to the high-riding canine I never found out. I hope they did and that the dog was unharmed from the driver's ignorance. Both situations also make me wonder if black labs are really more defiant and predisposed to independence. Could it be a coincidence? Maybe, or perhaps, in the case of these two dogs, the owners were not playing with a full deck of cards.

Keep Your Paws inside the Exit Door at All Times

Tazz, our Germador, has been growing rapidly and at a still young age of five months, he has grown to a robust fifty pounds. Baby Girl, now thirteen months, is still the same height and weight since we had first gotten Tazz. Tazz can no longer walk under Baby Girl or the coffee table for that matter. Some things, however, haven't changed. On any given day in my household it is like a Saturday Night Fight on HBO.

Now their play fighting is mostly play and less like fighting, which is somewhat a load off of our shoulders. The casualties are no longer the fighters themselves, but common household items, from water bowls to doors, most specifically the side door of our modular home. The foundation sits about four feet off of the ground and exiting from this side door means a four foot drop to the ground.

It was almost Spring, St. Patrick's day to be exact, and one of the dogs did something to piss the other one off – badly. Sitting in my living room I heard the usual growling, barking, and running except this time it seemed more intense. I got up off of the couch and put my book down on the coffee table when the tumbling blur of white, gray, black, and brown went past me and down the hallway. The door was at the end of the hallway and had become tonight's victim. The blurry tornado hit the door with such force that it broke the lock and swung open.

With a thud!, a crash!, and a woof! Tazz fell out of the door and landed on the ground. I exclaimed a rather loud curse word and ran towards the door. By the time I took the few steps to get there Tazz was gone and Baby Girl stood there panting trying to catch her breath. I was instantly worried about Tazz and hastily went to the front door. Tazz was sitting on the front porch, wagging his tail in anticipation of coming back inside.

I opened the door and knelt down as my little Tazz man shook his doggy butt and licked my face. I was so worried in that instant when he fell that he ran out in the road or out to the woods. That was not the case and he was back in, thankfully. Baby Girl had hid in crate when I let Tazz back in the house, she must have thought that she would be reprimanded. The incident did not effect Tazz one bit and him and Baby Girl continued their play fighting, but with less intensity now. There was no punishment for either of them, just a lot of grateful hugs and a stronger lock.

A few weeks later the blurry tornado had struck again with paws of furry. With a forceful blow the new lock did not hold up and the door flew open again. This time it was Baby Girl that fell out. I was in the kitchen finishing up the dishes when I heard a loud thud and yelp. I rushed and saw Tazz standing near the open door looking down. I closed it and like clockwork went to the front porch. There was Baby Girl. She was given praise for coming in and the next day an even stronger lock had to be installed.

It is a pet owner's vital responsibility to take stock in the care and safety of their pets. I am thankful that I was home for these two episodes and took the necessary steps to remedy the problem, at least in part. I am also grateful that neither dog was injured and they both had the sense to come up on the porch immediately and return inside the house. A common and funny saying that Jason and I often use now is "Keep your paws inside the exit door at all times."

No Turtles Were Harmed...

Raising a puppy to be a well-balanced animal is sometimes easier said than done. Both of my dogs fit in with our family perfectly, it's when those occasions occur when we venture with our pets outside of our home when socialization becomes an issue. Some major nation-wide retail chain pet stores offer a pet open door policy. PetSmart and Petco are among the top that encourage and promote it.

Personally I have always liked the notion of going into those types of stores and seeing happy owners with their happy pets. I have never taken any of my previous dogs to those stores, but I wanted to try it. Jason was in agreeance and it was decided upon. We had had Baby Girl for a few months and it seemed like the right time to take her. However, we mistakenly chose a Saturday afternoon to go.

The four of us must have been a sight. Jason held Baby Girl's leash and the four of us, including Amber and myself, walked across the parking lot to the PetSmart entrance and in we went. It was a "first" for us as a family and it was thoroughly exciting. I had gotten a large red cart and strolled in like we owned the place; we were relaxed and at ease, that was our second mistake. Baby Girl has a good temper with us and for the most part other persons and dogs therefore we did not think twice; so far she showed no anxiety.

Our shopping list was small: dog food, rope toy, and a retractable leash. We just needed to get what we came for and before hand decided not to linger around longer than we needed. By the time we got a full dozen or so feet in the establishment Baby Girl's senses were being overloaded. This bright building brought so many new scents and eye candy. There were people with their dogs, animals (aquatic, small, and feline), food, treats, and toys all of which drove our canine into a frenzy.

Walking through the dead center of the store we passed aquatics and just like that Baby Girl pulled an exit-stage-left move and dashed into the small animal department which also contained birds. Oh how Baby Girl loves to bark at birds. Jason tightened his grip and reduced her slack, we kept moving.

"Why did she do that?" Amber asked.

"This is all new to her." Jason responded. Baby Girl was very happy and very hyper; her nose lead the way while her brain tried to keep up the constant changing and blending of smells.

This may not have been the best idea? I thought to myself when Baby Girl's first nose-to-nose encounter occurred near the pet carrier isle. It was with a Weimarner. The owner holding the real genuine leather strap leash was a man in his forties whom himself donned a Ralph Lauren Polo shirt. Not only was it a clash of the canines, but also of the social classes. Jason had a canine pedestal of sorts and the Weimarners were at the top. Their look and heritage never failed to impress.

"I like your dog." Jason said to the man as he held on to Baby Girl's leash for dear life. The man looked at Jason then down to the panting and prodding Husky which was eagerly trying to sniff his *Best In Show* canine's rear end. He scoffed and made no reply.

"Girl stop!" I said loudly as the Weimarner wanted nothing to do with having his butt sniffed.

The soft gray dog with bright blue eyes turned up his head with back-end following and planted it safely on the floor away from Baby Girl's nose. Taking the insult in the appropriate way our female canine barked loudly. The man and the best in show left the isle leaving us with a barking dog. Thankfully it wasn't worse and Baby Girl's short attention span allowed us to head off towards the dog food section. *Thank goodness.* I thought. No dogs in this isle which allowed us a short break.

Perusing the brands and sale tags the selected purchase was made, Puppy Chow, and it was placed in the red cart. Before leaving the isle a young blonde in her early twenties turned the corner. In one hand she daintily carried a shopping basket and on the opposite shoulder hung a black and pink bag with a tiny light brown and black furry head sticking out of the top. Amber's eyes widened at the sight of the tiny head with pink bow and asked the lady.

"What's your puppy's name?" The lady smiled and replied.

"Princess." Once Baby Girl saw Amber giving another dog attention that was it; it was on. Baby Girl was out of hyper drive and in protection mode.

Canine counter number two was worse than the first one. This time Baby Girl jumped, but luckily Jason held the leash tight enough and neither the woman nor princess was hit, just scared and nervous. I would be too. My dog could have eaten her dog as a snack. We moved on very quickly now through the rest of the store.

"Let's finish so we could get out of here." I was now as anxious as Baby Girl. Next to the toy and supplies section, we had only a rope toy and retractable leash to get. I tried to talk Jason into just leaving, but he refused.

"I like that little dog. Can we get one." Amber asked.

"No!" Jason and I both replied irately and simultaneously.

We didn't yell, but were both frustrated and made it clear to Amber that we were not getting a Yorkie. In return both our faces were as red now as the cart I pushed. We selected the leash with out any problem, no interruptions. Now the last and final item: the rope toy. *Oh no!* This isle was filled with dogs. We went with defensive measures this time and weaved our way around and I grabbed the cheapest rope toy on the shelf. It was if we were on one of those game shows where they do speed shopping and cart racing. She lunged at two other dogs, an Irish Terrier and a Welsh Springer Spaniel, gratefully Jason held on and debunked her efforts.

Finally, done!

We only had to check-out now. So far, so good. The line I chose wasn't the shortest, but more importantly, no dogs in the lane. The customers paid and slowly we moved up the line.

"At least we avoided the cats for adoption." Jason said happily and we all laughed and snickered. *That would have been a disaster.* It never came to be.

We were up now. "Oh what a beautiful Husky!" The smiling cashier had proclaimed.

"Thanks." I said in reply and was all smiles now. *We did it.* I thought, but I had thought too soon.

"Why are all the other dogs acting so good in the store and Baby Girl isn't?" Amber asked and in turn I explained about how each dog is different and went on about

171

socialization and so forth. Jason took the calm moment to look over towards the grooming department. Prepared with my debit card out and ready to pay the cashier and from behind me was yelling something indistinct about my dog. I was caught off guard; I looked at the lady then quickly down at Baby Girl.

"Oh no!" I exclaimed. By now Jason's attention was recaptured and horrifically I saw what was happening. She was squatting down and emptying her bowels.

Jason yanked on her leash and she let out a yelp and out the door they went. Everyone whom was up front saw what had happened and if they didn't see it they sure smelled it. My transaction was complete and now the smile was gone from the cashier's face and was replaced with a scowl. She extended her arms and handed me a baggie, spray bottle, and roll of paper towels.

Yep, my dog took a dump in PetSmart and I'm on my hands and knees cleaning it up off of the floor. I could feel my face getting hotter every second and I imagine that it looked ten shades redder than the cart did.

Most of the employees and customers where making comments and talking among themselves. I glanced up and noticed the man with the Weimarner scoffing and shaking his head. Likely the next lane over was the woman with her Yorkie. I think she actually took a picture of me with her camera phone. I finished and left as fast and abruptly as I could.

"Why couldn't she have done that in an inconspicuous part of the store where at least no one would have seen?" I asked myself out loud walking across the parking lot.

At least we were out of there – never to return.

Back at the car Jason sat in the driver's seat while Baby Girl occupied half the back and front paws extended on the arm rest. Amber and I got in and were greeted by a very long tongue licking me across the face. It was if Baby Girl was saying *Thanks for the field trip and cleaning up my mess mom. I feel much better now.* My anger melted and the humiliation eventually faded. We decided right then and there to better socialize any future dogs that we may have.

The following year Tazz was five months old and ready to go on his first public outing.

Here we go again. Thinking to myself.

"We need to socialize him before he gets too old." I reasoned with Jason. Neither of us wanted a repeat, but thought we should at least give Tazz a shot at it. This time I chose a Petco in the next town over on a Wednesday evening, just in case disaster would strike again.

We thought we were prepared for the unexpected, we were wrong. Though Tazz was still young he also weighed fifty pounds. He had a green harness, both his and my favorite color, which also afforded Jason more control. He had a short leash with a tight grip and in we went. Firstly, we had seen the sign in the front of the store. The Wednesday night obedience class was in process.

Wonderful! I thought. Grabbing a cart we headed straight to the dog food. "If things go bad get him out and I'll take care of the rest." Jason nodded at that and we proceeded with our game plan.

The dog food, Puppy Chow, is the only type of dog food that Baby Girl would eat. She turned her nose up at everything else and if she did eat another brand it usually did not agree with her. I was used to giving all my previous dogs Science Diet – Nature's Best. But Baby Girl would have none of it, so if it's good enough for her then it's good enough for him. Tazz had eaten everything from our bed mattress to rocks to goose poo without blinking an eye, Puppy Chow was definitely a step up.

No problems so far Tazz's anxiety level, it was low and he thoroughly enjoyed sniffing everything that came across his nose. We stopped at the dog treat bar and loaded up a bag of various treat selections. Tazz especially liked the dog treat bar. Amber snuck him a small yellow-colored dog biscuit which I was not pleased about and planned on talking to her about it after we left the store.

All was good.

"I'd like to look at the snakes." Jason said and headed with Tazz over to the aquatic animal department and Amber wanted to look at tarantulas. I shivered at the thought and bought a piece of aquatic background paper for the fish tank. The Beta was doing well and had a few new roommates, two snails one white and one black. I was proud of Tazz, he whined a few times and only barked once. He also enjoyed the fish section, watching them swim around was thrilling for him. Jason liked a particular corn snake with red and white markings and Amber wanted the hairy spider.

"No." I told each of them.

We were all happy the trip went well and were almost ready to leave. We passed a large black outdoor pond display which caught Tazz's attention. The mini waterfall and air filter made noise, but it wasn't that which drew Tazz's attention. It was the smell and sight of the green oval objects swimming beneath the waters surface. The display contained several red ear slider turtles. Jason allowed for a little slack so Tazz could smell the reptiles and he took them all in. Out of nowhere Tazz leapt into the air and landed in the pond with a monstrous splash. He resembled a long legged frog that sits completely still and jumps without warning and with substantial ease. This was now Tazz, he was in the water up to his waist and poking his nose at the sliders.

"Get him out!" I exclaimed at Jason.

He tugged, pulled, and yelled to no avail. The dog wouldn't move. All the commotion attracted customers who laughed, employees who were shocked, and one very mean looking store manager who hollered.

"Get your dog out of there now!" The manager yelled and Jason gave up pulling. He accepted the inevitable reaching over with both arms and scooping him out lifting vertically and setting Tazz on the now wet floor. He looked up at us with that cute look and dripped profusely; he then insisted on shaking the excess water off. Most of it got on the store manager whom let out another shout.

"Out!"

Jason left hurriedly with Tazz then the evil glare fixed now on me from the large burly-looking manager. I stuttered for a second. "I...I'm... going to pay for this." I pointed my finger downwards at the cart. "...then leave." Not saying another word I hurried off towards the cash registers with Amber following. Soon we were out of the store and instead of turning several shades of red and being embarrassed Amber and I looked at each other and laughed.

"That was so cool!" Amber exclaimed and in reply I stated. "At least none of the turtles were hurt." We both laughed harder.

Jason stood near the car; he was letting Tazz drip dry on the pavement. By now the employees had it all mopped up and at least we gave the pet store some excitement for the day. Jason looked disappointed.

"That couldn't have gone any better." He scoffed. Tazz was more his dog than mine and he expected more from him. "Well, Tazz likes green. What can I say." This time the humiliation was his when he walked out being just as drenched as his dog was.

"At least you didn't have to clean poop up in front of twenty people starring and taking pictures of you." I replied smiling. He knew I was right, that was worse.

The result of both take-your-pet-shopping-with-you adventures turned out to be same. We have two wonderful dogs that love their family, dislike other dogs, and one in particular has an undeniable interest in turtles.

Office Pets

It was a mid-morning Friday late in June. The accounting office was at half staff of employees, but doubles the amount of canines. It was National Take Your Pet to Work Day. As the day progressed the normal amount of phone calls were received and clients were in and out as usual. Despite the normality it was like the Wild West, somewhat deserted and hostile. The meetings and deadlines pressed on with no regard to the day of week or national status of this day. The day was interesting and cumbersome with lots of surprises – and fur!

The two-floor brick with green trim respectable-looking building held all sorts of financial advisors, accountants, insurance agents, and clerks. In addition to these roles there were the four-legged furry side kicks as well on this particular day.

Most offices were stationed on the second floor. Tawny, a robust and vibrant fifty-year old tax advisor, couldn't pass up on the association's first welcomed Take Your Pet to Work Day. She had brought her Smooth Collie; their hair in color tone almost matched perfectly. Each had red, blonde, and a tinge of brown streaming through long-length hair which fit each of their personalities perfectly – sassy and vibrant.

The month prior Tawny and Marmalee, her Collie, were invited to a doggy birthday party. She had brought pictures into work the following week and shown everyone. The party was puppy picture perfect and was complete with party hats, a homemade doggy cake, and treat bags for the party-goers. According to Tawny it is an experience that every dog and owner should have. Personally, with my dogs, they would be the party crashers. I think I'd pass on the event.

Kristy, an accountant and the computer guru, brought in Moron. He was a four-year old male Pug. Kristy had quite the sense of humor in choosing his name and as far as accountants go she has far more of an imagination than others have. Moron was cute and intelligent for a pug with a name that no matter how much he tried he could not live down.

Moron was secured with a long blue leash and spent most of the day looking around, chewing on a dehydrated pig ear, Yum!, and laying on his big blue doggy bed. He was quite content for a dog and was happy to be near Kristy as much as possible.

Another office belonged to Sue; she was the company's insurance agent. Car, home, life, you name it and she sold it. I think she was even looking into getting licensed to sell pet insurance last I knew. She was vicious and direct and often made a lot of noise at work, just as her pet Chihuahua did, Jessy. They both had a strong and sharp temper and the matching short black hair to go along. The majority of the day Jessy stood on Sue's window ledge and barked. She must have been barking at the birds that flown too close to Sue's yellow Dodge Charger, make that Jessy's yellow Dodge Charger. Early in the morning Tawny had placed a post-it-note on Sue's door that read: *Guard Dog on Duty!* It almost got as many laughs as Moron did.

The office squarely in the middle of the second floor was Dawn's, the payroll specialist. She brought along Bobby. He was an Australian Shepherd; this was another case of dog's looking like their owners – isn't that the truth. Both had medium-length hair of mixed colors, tints, and highlights. Bobby could have been a Calico if he really wanted to. Dawn had stuck up a baby gate at the entrance to her office, which was not really needed since Bobby slept the entire day under Dawn's desk happily at her feet.

Four of the eight upstairs offices had workers and canines – the other four employees were off for one reason or another, but all owned dogs. Carrie Lyn, the accountant supervisor, often worked from home. That was the case on this Friday; she stayed at home with her two sons and Kipper and Moose, both English Mastiffs. They were a large family with large dogs.

Carl, the youngest and handsomest of all accountants, was home as well. He had taken time off to study for his upcoming CPA board exam. He later that day would take Charles, his Boston Terrier, to the dog park and play Frisbee. Margie, the accounting clerk, was off as well. Her family had a mini vacation planned at home for the weekend and kicked off the warm weather with her husband, son, daughter, and Border Collie, Esper, at the beach.

The last upstairs office was Caroline's. She was the vice-president and co-owner of the company. Having that status and also being a senior accountant her and her husband, also the company's owner took off on a vacation every few months. Caroline was home packing for their Alaskan cruise and getting ready to drop off their two Italian Greyhounds at Leisure Country Kennel and Spa. The two dogs were VIP's and their last stay occurred when their owners had flown to Orlando for the week and visited Disney World. These two lucky dogs were going to be pampered for six days and seven nights while Caroline and Venchensio did whale watching and took pics with their Cannon extra-long zoom lens camera.

Venchensio's office was downstairs. He was the owner and heart and soul of the company. For a financial advisor, investor, and accountant he had quite the sense of humor. It was almost the strange type of humor that paramedics have, if you have every known a paramedic. But instead of emergency care and treatment you had an investor whom liked the stock market as a paramedic liked vehicle accidents. Both professions are a strange breed. Venchensio had an office on the first floor. It was large, spacious, and complete with wide expansion windows and a flat panel television. No doubt the Italian-married couple was finishing packing for their trip and was also preparing their Italian dogs for their trip as well.

The other large office on the first floor was Cameron's. He was a partner in the company as well not to mention was Venchensio and Caroline's son. He was off on this Friday as well and attending an investment seminar in Philly. Being a dog lover as everyone in the company was he had a Malamute, Gracey, whom was at home with Cameron's wife and their two sets of twins: One identical set both being five-year old girls and the other set being both newborn twin identical boys. Their family was expanding so rapidly they could barely keep up, it's good for them they only have one dog.

Claudine was the only person working downstairs. She was the receptionist and was a spunky for the young age of sixty. She owned a white Toy Poodle and a Great Pyrenees. It was the clash of the canines sometimes, but she felt fortunate that she had the best of both worlds which also matched her personality. A little bit of feistiness meets strength and superiority. Though she loved and wanted to bring one of her dogs, she willfully kept them at home and respectfully did her job. She did it well as she was the glue which helped hold the company together.

The company canine turnout wasn't bad. All the dogs were well behaved and socialized. Claudine came upstairs around ten-thirty that morning and bellowed down the hallway.

"Fresh pot of coffee is ready and Mrs. Stanford stopped by with a box of cookies!" Well, most of them took off downstairs in search of sugar and caffeine. By afternoon most of the office personnel are on their third can of soda anyways.

Claudine poked her head in Dawn's door and inquired.

"Is he still sleeping?" Dawn didn't even have to look down under her desk. Her pumps were off and she could feel Bobby's fur under her hose covered feet.

Dawn replied to her and gave a cheerful. "Yep." Then she kept typing.

Claudine didn't venture upstairs too often as she had to watch the front door for visitors so when she did she often hurried. Her last stop before heading back down was to visit

Sue's office. The growling and barking of yippy and yappy continued furiously as Claudine approached. She had seen the post-it and laughed surprisingly.

"Stop that barking!" Sue shouted towards Jessy.

"Well at least he's in good company." Claudine remarked before heading back downstairs.

The most exciting and humorous moment of the day occurred when Moron had decided to escape from Kristy's office. He was too quiet and sneakily chewed through the blue nylon leash and was biding his time for the right moment. Just after lunch is when he made his move. The mid-afternoon coffee break was over and he must have been in need of relief himself because the light furry dog with blackened face ran and moved his little legs as fast as he could down the hallway.

"Moron! Get back here!" Kristy had shouted and ran after him.

The other upstairs employees all heard the commotion and looked out of their offices. Moron was fleeing to the end off the hallway when he stopped and spotted the eggshell colored base of the water cooler; it wasn't a red fire hydrant, but it would suffice none the less. He found his destination to which he was now going to relieve himself, and he did.

"Moron stop!" Kristy's face was red and she made a quick detour to the restroom and emerged with a roll of paper towels and cleaning spray. By now he was pleased and trotting back to his doggy bed in her office. Everyone had gotten a good laugh except for Kristy whom now was cleaning the mess then returned to her desk looking beet-red. She afforded him a few potty breaks, but she guessed that it had been one too short.

"Bad Moron." She said more calmly as she sat back behind her desk again.

All in all the day went well and as the end of the day grew nearer the offices emptied out one by one, canines loaded up and headed home. Claudine was the last to leave today as she was everyday. She locked the doors and closed up the building for the night. Part of her regretted not bringing one of her dogs and the other part didn't. She thought of Moron's transgression then thought. "At least it's only one day a year."

The Escape Artist

"Where in the heck did that dog go?!" Bobby McCain coarsely commented while he looked out the kitchen window and again the dog had disappeared. Flustered, Bobby exited the kitchen, went through the mud room, and out the back door onto the deck. When he opened the door his dog was sitting right there waiting for him, as always. Mason was a Husky, the wild-tailed six year-old Siberian Husky just sat there looking up at him. His tongue was hanging out the right side of his mouth panting feverishly. His expression said it all by giving the "Can I come inside with you dad?" look.

"Mason." Bobby's voice was stern yet trusting as he knew that Mason was a good dog and never took off when he escaped. Bobby couldn't help but to feel sorry for his canine as living in North Carolina brought miserable heat indexes and all that thick fur added to the misery. The dog drank all of his water and was fighting against dehydration and was a loss for the company of his people.

Mason was an outdoor dog. At first he had a dog house in a simple fenced-in yard. It did not take long for him to either dig his way out or muster up a good speed and obtained a running distance in order to clear the four-foot fence. When that failed a long leash was used. This did not work either as Mason was intelligent enough to chew through the nylon leash. Idea number three ended up as using a thicker cable-made leash. This challenge gave Mason new ideas to tackle and soon figured out how to wiggle his head and slip it out of his collar.

The McCain's were running out of options and their latest plan was to keep Mason in the garage. They always kept all the windows open and a large fan and let it run to keep the dog as cool as possible. Mason had a lot of amenities in the garage. A self gallon-sized replenishing water bowl, very nice, and a large royal blue plush doggy bed which matched the royal blue Porsche that was parked in the garage, also very nice. Even though Mason did not live in the air-conditioned house his doggy apartment was luxurious enough, complete with a hammock and ramp and a large assortment of chewies and toys. Oh, don't forget about the blue-camo pattered pup tent also. The McCain's had spared no expense.

Bobby was walking Mason back to the garage and passed the outside pool which had a doggy ramp for easy access in and out of the pool.

"Overkill." He thought every time he'd seen it. It was Jessica's idea, his wife. Most of the dog's luxury items were her doing. She loved the dogs and wanted them to have the best.

While Mason had his living quarters outside, the family had another dog that lived inside the house, Clover. He was a pampered two-year old Chihuahua. Getting him was also Jessica's idea as he was not too fond of his yappiness. Clover was a gift for the kids and he had gotten the better end of the deal. A small dog with hardly any fur would do better out in the garage than a large dog with a load of fur.

"Don't you be trying to get out again." Bobby checked all the windows and closed the garage door shut. He was still perplexed on how he'd done it. He did notice one of the windows was up slightly higher than usual, but he wasn't sure if indeed Mason was wrangling his way out the window.

"Na..." He temporarily dismissed the thought when Jess and the kids pulled up the drive in their Explorer.

"What's up?" She got out and asked him. He had a questioning look on his face.

"Our escape artist was at it again. That darn dog gets out of everything."

"Again?" She replied in question.

"Yeah. I'm going to keep an eye out. I think he's lifting up that window and jumping out." He motioned over to the garage window.

Jess looked at him in disbelief. "No way." She had also dismissed the idea, but unlike him she did not give it another thought and went inside the house. She thought it was impossible; he didn't.

Over the next few days he'd paid more attention and kept watch. Mason kept escaping and it was always when Bobby was not looking. For three days straight Bobby was not able to obtain any proof and he was getting flustered. So far he had faltered more than the dog did. He had enough and was determined to catch Mason in the act, so on the forth day he decided it was time for video surveillance.

"Oh yeah." Bobby spoke to himself. "This will get him." He stood on a ladder in the garage and was screwing in a video camcorder to the wall. It was pointing towards the window in question. It was the window on the left hand side, just above the work bench.

"What are ya doing?" Jess asked.

"Installing this here camcorder." He replied and continued to explain. "I think he's jumping up on the workbench then sticking his head out the window and lifting it up." He spoke sequentially and used his arms and hands to explain step by step how the dog managed his escape maneuvers.

Jess looked at him as he was categorizing every step, but she did not respond or make any sound. She just stood there arms folded and the expression on her face was that of someone looking at a red light. It was an unemotional and waiting-for-it-to-change expression. But he didn't falter in response to her lack of response. She just sighed and walked back into the house. She knew he had his mind fixated on this no matter what she said or what she did. She was fed up with the whole theory of Mason and the window.

Bobby knew Jess well enough to know that she needed proof, and not just an eye witness account, actual proof. He was going to get it. He hummed enthusiastically and completed the last adjustments to the recording system. Mason sat next to him looking up happily, tongue still hanging out of his mouth. He had an expression which said. "Is all of this for me?" Mason was all about getting attention from his people and they never failed to disappoint. Bobby however, in this endeavor, didn't want to draw attention to himself and wanted to keep a low profile. "Bobby McCain, P.I." He thought and smiled inwardly.

Two hours later dusk was setting in. Bobby was peeled to the kitchen window waiting. No movement. He was loosing interest and being distracted by the tv. The Braves were playing. "Bottom of the fifth…" He heard from the other room. The game was on and he was missing it. The tv was up as loud as Jess would permit it, but no matter he still wasn't in his recliner watching it with an energy drink or soda in hand.

He was fed up for the night. He did just what he wanted, he got up and got himself a can and was going to watch the game. Just as he cracked it open he looked out the window one last time. His eyes widened when he'd seen a small black object poking out of the window.

He sat back down, sipped his beverage, and watched with a freshly-peaked interest. His attention drowned out the background noise from the game.

"This is it!" He thought. The black object moved side to side then up a bit. It would retreat in for a moment then poke back out. The cycle was repeated a few times, each time the window went up more and more. Finally Mason's head poked out.

"Got him!" Bobby yelled bursting with excitement. There was just enough space and Mason took advantage of it and squeezed through in the space allotted. It was all he needed and it only took him a few seconds to jump down and run up on the deck.

"Yes. I was right." He was gleaming and by the time he got to the door and there was Mason waiting for him, tail thumping on the wood deck planks and as always with tongue hanging out.

"Whoo-hoo!" He shouted sounding like an American version of the *Crocodile Hunter*. He was happy to see Mason sitting there. There was no scolding or shaming just a pat on the head given. Mason happily followed Bobby as he went to retrieve the tape. Jess and the kids were on the deck now taking in all the commotion.

"Mason got out and I got it on tape!" He exclaimed.

"I can't believe he really jumped out through that window!" Jess was amazed and Bobby wanted to rub it in her face that he was right. He didn't have to say it, he knew that she knew that he was right.

Five minutes later they were all in the living room, dogs included, and were rewinding the tape. Bobby had rewound too far and in his excitement had taped over the second half of a Christmas special. Oops. His youngest protested about the loss of the Christmas show, but soon got over it as they watched Mason squeezing through the window.

They all laughed and decided to send the tape into one of those shows that play funny videos on tv. It would be televised for sure. The next question was what to do now? Mason would surely keep getting out and they deliberated on whether to install a more sturdy lock, moving the work bench, or putting in a heavy-duty screen in the window.

The next day the work bench was moved.

The following day Mason got out again.

Bobby McCain, P.I. is back on the job.

Job Title: The Escape Artist

On the Wild Side

Wolves, Coyotes, and Their Domestic Mixes

Though wolves and coyotes are beautiful wild animals they are none the less still that – wild. Most domestic breeds have been domesticated centuries ago to live with and interact with humans versus their wild counterparts whom are still wild.

Wolves, coyotes and domestic dogs can breed in the wild, but this happens very seldom. "The wolf, *Canis lupus* and the dog, *Canis familiaris* can and do breed and produce offspring." This cross is called a wolf-dog. People often have the misconception that a mix between the two animals would produce a superior animal being domesticated, trainable, strong, and beautiful.

This is not the case and the mixing of the *Canis,* it can only mean trouble. "Nature has selected for the wolf traits that ensure its survival in the wild: aggression, caution, suspicion, self-protection; none of the traits we want in our dogs."

Wolf-dog crosses, even with a small amount such as one-quarter, still contain wolf genetics and pose a danger in living in close quarters with people. The choice in wolf-dogs and coyote-dogs, including breeding the species, should be avoided completely.

In Jason's youth he had an all too close and traumatic experience with a wolf-dog crossbreed. He recalls every detail to this day and will never forget.

When he was twelve years old him and his father, Jason Senior, had went a few counties to the north and east to see a Native American friend, Tribesman. Tribesman lived in a hand built cabin with his wife and two children, and their wolf-dog. Being of pure Native American descent the family faithfully upheld all the traditional believes.

Jason Senior at the time had a lot of respect for Tribesman and their heritage. Jason Jr. on the other hand, was almost a teenager and full of curiosity. He had never met a Native American and was in wonder by the cabin, the family, the property, and the surrounding woods. So off he went to explore with Tribesman and Jason Senior long behind him following in discussion. Jason had walked the front of the cabin and rounded the corner and began walking towards the rear of the property.

There was a fire pit, homemade spear, garden, and a wood bridge that spanned a small creek. That's where Jason decided to head to. In the friendship of the two adults, Tribesman had failed to mention his wolf-dog which Jason had seen and irreversibly woke up. Jason saw the animal in his area. A food and water dish next to a shed and the animal laying on a large older blanket on the ground. Jason noticed there was no leash, no collar, and the blackish-blue eyes were now fully open and staring at him. Jason stopped and was silent. He could hear the indistinct chattering of his father and Tribesman behind him a ways back.

Jason redirected his attention to the animal that was slowly rising off of his hind legs, yet his front legs where still lowered. He was hunched and Jason felt a sinking feeling in his stomach; it was awful terrible feeling that stirred in him as the animal remained unmoved and silence for the following few seconds. Those eyes remained on him and something just clicked inside of Jason snapped. His fight-or-flight instinct kicked in.

Stay or run? Jason thought and in a split second decision, right or wrong, he turned and ran.

Jason senior and Tribesman both looked up when they heard a fast rustling coming from around the corner of the cabin. They both took off running knowing it was probably Jason. The same time they took off to run was about the same time that the wolf-dog had leapt up and took off a small lacerating chunk of Jason's right arm. Jason kept going despite the laceration and luckily Tribesman and Jason's father reached the wolf-dog before it had a chance to attack again.

All hollered and the two adults did their best to get the animal under control. Tribesman was perplexed that their wolf-dog attacked as he had never done that before.

Jason ran in the cabin and the wife and daughter immediately rinsed and wrapped his wounded arm. Jason sobbed for only a minute from the pain; he was tougher than that to let an animal make him get upset. Tribesman's son when outside to help his father and Jason senior. The wolf-dog was subdued and put in the shed. Jason senior was understandably upset over the incident and unfortunately it had ended their friendship.

Jason healed fine he was lucky the wolf-dog did not do anymore damage than what was already done. This was the first and only time that he was bitten by a dog and he has the permanent scar on his arm to remind him that wild animals are wild no matter what. The trauma did not affect him for long, two years later his family adopted Princess and had gotten Milo and Jake.

Any wolf or coyote researcher would tell you that "Wild is wild no matter what". I am directly quoting a coyote researcher from a lecture that I was in attendance at for an environmental biology class at Edinboro University. The speaker and researcher was my cousin who is an eco-feminist and coyote advocate. She has done research in areas all over the country on coyotes, from state parks in Pennsylvania to the Rocky Mountains in Montana.

Coyotes live in every part of the Unites States and in both rural and urban areas. I recall recently listening to a Pittsburgh, PA radio station where a man had shot a coyote in his backyard.

She has lived with and observed many aspects of coyotes behaviors, including buy not limited to living and hunting in packs, mating, nutrition, offspring rearing, and most recently the migration and tracking of coyotes. She often leads a team who goes out into the dens and traps and tags coyotes. They have tracked members of the same coyote pack whom can travel up to seventy miles within range of their home den.

As most coyote and wolf researchers, would tell anyone that "wild is wild" and coyotes, wolves, or cross-breeds are not able to be domesticated animals and are not meant to be pets.

The Trespasser

It was a cold May morning and Bob Shaw got his paper off the front porch as he did every morning. He brewed his coffee and sat on the back deck as he did most mornings, blocking out the sun and trying to wake up. He had a decent sized backyard for living south east of downtown Pittsburgh.

Most of his yard was fenced in except for the west side of the property. A high row of thick hedges was the border and divider between his property and his neighbor's property. There were also numerous flowering bushes of Rhododendron, Chrysanthemums, and Hyacinths. The purple and pinkish flowers were enough to make him nauseous. There was also a Cherry Tree and a bird bath right in the middle of the yard. All of which were Pepper's doing, his second wife.

He heard the morning birds and sat on the too comfy patio furniture. He glanced up from his sports section with his disconcerted muddy brown eyes and glared at the bird bath.

"Darn birds. They'd look better up on my wall." Though he was speaking aloud to himself he flatly directed his comment to the male Cardinal, but it had fallen on bird ears and did him no good. He could threaten all he wanted, but it never got anywhere. He clicked his lower jaw and raised the paper up redirecting his attention back to the Pirate's stats.

Darn woman. He thought to himself. The fancy flowers, furnature, bird baths, it was all her doing. *And that prissy dog too...* He disliked Pepper Jr. just as much as Pepper herself. Pepper Jr. was a purebred Bedlington Terrier. He was white and had curly hair and a high-rise shape head. He was different for a dog, but none the less won Best In Show three years running at the Pittsburgh dog show.

Pepper Jr. came through the doggy door and stepped graciously on the back deck. He walked right past Bob and never gave him a second look. Pepper Jr. dutifully did his business back near the bird bath. He did the all-too-funny grass flicking with his back legs like most dogs do after nature takes it course, then he headed in. Trotting with his head held high like only the best of the best do. *Snobby dog.* Bob thought.

Finally Bob was able to finish his coffee and article and got ready for work. Luckily for Bob work was in his garage and his basement. He was a taxidermist – the best in the city. Being rough and touch and dealing with blood, guts, and gore he never understood why he married Pepper. She was the complete opposite of him. He supposed since he was the best that he wanted the best in a spouse and that was Pepper. She was younger, blonde, very attractive, and smart. *She's perfect.* He often thought.

Pepper was well educated and had taste. She was a new age girl and tried every fad out there from Yoga to Botox. She had Pepper Jr. specifically bred and trained to be a show dog, he was also the best. Her newest fad was studying Dogology. It's based on people's dispositions and interactions with their dogs. She had the book, visited the website, and signed up to be an advocate. Pepper did whatever she liked and put her mind to. She was a high-spirited individual. She liked Bob's rough and tough attitude, but she viewed herself being in charge of the household.

Bob was ready for work and headed out through the backyard towards his garage. A chipmunk had darted out

from underneath the Chrysanthemum bush and nearly
scared Bob half to death.

"Geez!" He exclaimed and jumped back about a foot
and a half. "What the?..."

Bob seen the flowering bushes still moving along with the
hedges directly behind it. He thought it was odd and
obviously something larger than the chipmunk was moving
back there. He didn't have time and didn't care. He hoped it
would be a cat that would take care of the chipmunk and
maybe even those birds next time.

Chipmunks are easy to stuff... He thought and that
was the end of it. He had bigger things to stuff. He was
working on a bobcat for a client. He walked over to the
freezer and pulled out his next project. It was full of fine
specimens that clients from all over the region brought to his
business. The bob cat was shot in New York State, the
southern tier, and was brought four hours south to him to be
worked on. Like he said he was the best.

Over the next few days as he finished up the bobcat
Bob noticed Pepper Jr. making a fuss over that flowering
bush and hedge. It would shake and sway sometimes, mostly
early morning and later in the evening, and Pepper Jr. would
bark and run. He didn't think much of it and he didn't like
that dog let alone want to give it any attention. As much as
he tried to dismiss it Bob couldn't help but notice how
persistent the dog was being.

"That dog is going to get its block knocked off." He
mumbled and headed out to the dog and the bush behind his
garage angrily.

"What is it?!" He yelled and Pepper Jr. backed off.

Bob got down on this hands and knees and swatted around underneath the bushed with his hands in hopes to deter whatever was under there. No movement followed after he was finished. He sensed there was something under there, but left it alone.

"Now you better shut up." Bob spoke in the direction of the dog and went back into his garage and closed the doors.

Later that evening Bob was sitting on his back porch, as most often did, when his neighbor arrived home next door. His name was Lance Shaw, no relation. Bob, of course, did not like Lance as he did not like many people.

"Hey there neighbor!" Lance raised his hand and waved and Bob waved in return, but gave no greeting. Bob had hoped that Lance could just go inside, but he wasn't that lucky. Lance came walking over.

"Pepper Jr. has been making a big deal about the bushes back there. Is everything all right?" Lance asked and was generally concerned. He was a studious one, A professor at Penn State, biology department. He also loved dogs and dog shows. *Pepper should have married this guy.* Bob thought, but did not repeat aloud.

"Yeah. Something was back there in and out for a few days. Don't know what. I think I scared it off today." Lance nodded listening and was just being neighborly. He knew that Bob did not care for him much and in turn he intently disliked him being a taxidermist and his field of specialty was dogs, both wild and domestic. Both were complete opposites. After a brief conversation Bob had retired in front of the HD TV and put on the sports channels.

195

"Darn dog biologist." He mumbled and cracked open his beer.

That evening the rustling in the bushes continued in small spurts, it had not gone unnoticed by Lance whom was working outside with his two large Mastiffs. The dogs had noticed and were acting oddly. They would sniff rapidly being drawn closer to the bushes and the scents which seemed so intriguing one second and then were driven off by instinct into retreat mode. Lance did not want to venture too far into the bushes and find himself in a possible unpleasant encounter with a raccoon or a possum. He did what any good biologist did. He observed, documented, and reported.

Lance did not want to waste his time dealing with Bob. Pepper was much more agreeable in terms of neighborliness and concern for the well being of the dogs. He had more in common with Pepper than with Bob.

The following morning was the same as the previous ones. The brush was intermittently swaying, dogs barking, and finally Bob had reached his breaking point. He loaded his long rifle and was going to take care of the problem himself, today. Lance wasn't home to meddle and Pepper was at a fashion show downtown. That had left himself and Pepper Jr. *I've got plenty of time to take care of this.* He thought malignantly.

The rifle made the cocking noise and Pepper Jr. hit the ground running. He had a spasm quality to his movement, but who could blame him. His irate owner had a gun and he did not want to be around or worse the target of Bob's fury.

Bob was psyched; he'd been watching too many hunting shows lately on his flat panel and he was determined to get the animal. He snuck around the yard looking like Snoopy

196

imitating the Red Barron. Due to Bob's short attention span he decided he'd have enough waiting around for the animal to show itself and went for the more direct approach. He was going in. He set the rifle against the side of the garage and found his assault weapon of choice, a large rake. He needed to flush it out first and then shoot it.

Pepper Jr. sat warily in the adjacent front corner of the fenced-in yard. Bob refused to let the dog inside and had hoped the animal was large and maybe would go for Pepper Jr. *Two birds, one stone.* The wickedly thought and smiled inwardly.

Bob had been right. The rake was effective and with one swiftly forceful blow underneath the brush and the trespasser was forced out.

"Holy crap!" Bob exclaimed and was knocked backwards by the charging animal. It was an eastern coyote. Male, large, and was now ticked off. He was forced out against his will and was now surveying the area.

Bob froze, but was slowing getting to his feet and decided to rush for his gun. The coyote eyed the shaking and yelping terrier in the corner and decided to go for it.

Yes! He's taking the bait. Pepper Jr. was the bait in question and the coyote was swiftly moving towards him. Bob contemplated for a moment whether or not he should let the animal take the intended bait. But in the end he did the right thing and protected the dog. Besides he knew that the consequences from his wife would be more severe than the damage that any coyote could inflict.

The coyote lunged and Bob fired. The shot was dead on, literally. It struck the coyote squarely in the chest, mid rib cage, and straight through the heart.

"Yes!" He was overjoyed and the coyote was dead instantly from the impact and only lay three feet in front of the terrier. The Best in Show had too much excitement and darted for the back door.

"Whoo-hoo!" Bob lifted the coyote checking its head and appendages. He was quite pleased with himself. *A fine trophy.* Bob was even forgetting his temper toward the show dog and looked up on the porch and yelled towards Pepper Jr. "I got it boy!" Pepper Jr. did not care and only wanted the lady of the house and his plush doggy bed.

Bob snapped pictures with his cell phone and called Chris, his best friend. By now attention from the gunshot was starting to pick up. Neighbors called the police and a crowd was gathering in the driveway. Pepper had arrived home first.

"What's going on?" She walked up looking perplexed and saw the brown, white, and dark mixed colored animal laying on the driveway.

"Is that a dog?" She asked, but was careful not to get too close.

"No. It's a coyote." Bob said, walked over smiling a wicked smile, and put his arm around his wife.

"Here in Pittsburgh. You shot a coyote?" She asked but didn't quite believe it.

"Yep. Right here in the backyard." He was more pleased with himself by the second as the crowd grew. There were reporters, camera crews, and the teenager down the block was making a video to post on YouTube. He was quite proud of himself, but Pepper did not view the situation the same way and neither did Lance who arrived home two hours after the event occurred. Now the police showed up along with the game commission.

"What do we have here?" He commission officer asked as he walked up through the parting crowd and looked at the dead bleeding coyote lay on the driveway.

"Sir it's illegal to fire a weapon in Allegheny County residential areas." The uniformed municipal officer informed Bob.

His jaw dropped an inch and he responded to the two officers. "But, it was going to attack my dog." He spoke the truth, but that's not why he shot the trespassing animal. He wanted to stuff it and mount it and torment Pepper and Pepper Jr. with it. Not once in the two hours following did it ever occur to Bob that what he did was illegal or wrong.

"I'm going to have to fine you and fill out a report. It's going to up to the district justice whether or not the charges of firing your weapon will be dealt with." The municipal officer relayed to Bob whom could not believe his ears. He was a hero, or so he thought. He should be commended, not fined. Apparently the law and most of the population did not agree with him and his actions.

The game commissioner now spoke up. "Sir we are going to have to confiscate your rifle as well. Once the D.J. rules on your case then it may be returned to you."

Bob was outraged, but did surrender the rifle to the officer. What else could he do, tell them no? He wanted to tell them a lot worse than that, but cooperated hesitantly.

Now Lance was over with the crowd that was slowly dispersing,

"Nice Bob. Really Nice." He flatly said with his arms crossed firmly against his chest. Pepper was inside as she couldn't watch the mob any longer as her husband was the ringleader of it.

The YouTube broadcast was a huge hit. Within forty-eight hours there were over sixty thousand hits. The news casts and print news were not as glorious to Bob and his actions. He was portrayed as a callus man whom with a gun posed more of a threat than the poor defenseless coyote did. It was the truth.

Life was relatively the same. The judge placed a large fine on Bob Shaw for his actions and was sentence to a formidable gun training course and fifty hours of community service in a state park. The outrage and heated forums that this event had caused for the city were now dwindling down and most activists agreed with the punishment, after all people cannot just go around the city shooting animals.

Bob stuffed that trespasser and even though he had a small sentence he fulfilled it. The coyote was mounted in his den. Pepper Jr. refused to enter that room ever again; he knew it gave Bob joy from his fear. Pepper also hated it, as did Lance, which never saw it but knew it was in there. Lance had often thought trespasser or not it was no excuse to shoot it and stuffing it was even worse. Pepper hated it as well, but she was grateful that Bob did not let it attack her baby, the Best in Show.

The Coyote Wild

The first time Ann saw a coyote she was astonished beyond belief. She reached down and grabbed Dean's hand and gave it a firm squeeze.

"Oh my God! What is it eating?" she said exasperatedly.

"Don't know." Dean replied bluntly. They both had stood there wide-eyed and bewildered.

The newly-wed couple lived adjacent to the woods that they were now crouching down in. Until recently they had lived in the suburbs all their life, but now had bought a home in the country of western Pennsylvania. This area of woods was dense and vast being next to a large lake and two state parks; 13,000 plus acres of wilderness paradise. Bears were not uncommon and neither were coyotes, but neither Ann nor Dean had seen one until today.

"That's grotesque, but intriguing..." Ann's voice trailed off as the small coyote pup ripped its meal apart; limb-from-limb, literally. Dean had thought it looked like the remains of a rabbit. The pup was small, maybe three or four months old, and alone.

Undoubtfully, the mother or father coyote were not far off probably watching the two of them. They hid behind a large rock. They were down wind, but it didn't provide much protection.

"Coyotes will eat just about anything honey, including garbage." He informed Ann. She had barely paid him any mind. Her eyes were fixated on the small coyote. His coat was a mixture of white, gray, and sable. Ann though that he had the most adorable blue tinted eyes and he was indescribably cute; it had made her heart melt. Yet, he was none the less a wild animal she reminded herself as he continued to devour his meal.

They were both excited at the first sighting and hoped that it would not be their last. The previous week Ann, Dean, and their daughter Marie were in the local borough's library. An older librarian and two patrons, donned in Carhart's and camo outfits, were discussing coyotes in the area. A few dogs that were chained up and left alone were attacked and killed by coyotes. The occurrences were fairly close to where Ann and Dean lived, two to five miles north. Dean remembered this conversation while kneeling and watching the coyote pup.

There was a rustling in the snowy brush about fifty yards off to the west. Dean reached around and grasped his .22 long rifle. He pulled it off of his shoulder strap and took it off of safety. Both were alarmed and the pup had taken off towards the brush. Ann and Dean assumed it was his parents, but were not sure.

"Let's go. Quietly." Dean said.

"Good idea." Ann replied.

Ann got up first and led the way. Dean followed briskly behind her. They followed the snow covered path to the left back towards their house. They stood out against the white snow covered background wearing their fluorescent orange and camouflage gear. Once they were out of the woods and had breached the large field behind their house they had breathed a sigh of relief.

Ann was enthralled. "That was unbelievable honey! Good thing we didn't have the dogs with us. They would have spooked him for sure." They had slowed their pace considerably now since they were almost back and out of immediate danger.

"If they took down a chained dog just think what they could do to our puppies." Dean said and shook his head in attempt to block the image of the rabbit from his mind as they continued to walk towards their back door.

There was a winter-weather advisory that night and the large fluffy flakes settled on the ground and accumulated busily. Dean, Ann, and Marie spent most of the night next to the fire place in the living room. Since it was Friday night the pizza and pop went almost as fast as their two dogs scarfed down their bowls of puppy food. Their puppies Bashful and Dopey, both Yellow labs, were soon fast asleep after they ate. All in the household, including the two dogs, perked up when they heard howling in the distance, soon followed by barking, and faint voices. Dean got up and looked out the back window, but saw nothing. They had all dismissed the noises and retired for the night.

By the end of the snow-filled episode nearly six inches of new snow fell on the ground. The next morning Dean had laced up his boots in anti-anticipation of shoveling.

"It could've been worse – I guess." He had said sarcastically. Ann wanted to go back out in the woods this afternoon in hopes of seeing another coyote though the thought of seeing an adult would be both shocking and sublime. Ann had patted Bashful on the head admiringly before she had zipped up her coat. She wanted to take the dogs, but feared they would scare off a coyote.

"Sorry guys not this time." The two dog's tails had beat eagerly against the kitchen tile and she had closed the door. Ann met up with Dean in the rear of the driveway and they started their three-mile hike back through the woods.

During their trek Dean stopped dead in his tracks and raised his right arm to stop Ann. "What's wrong?" She said and she turned to the left side to see what Dean had been gasping at. A pack of coyotes had taken down a dog. It was a large Shetland Collie from what they could tell. It was the dog from next door.

"It must have gotten loose last night." Dean said as quietly as possible.

"Ah!" Ann exclaimed and grimaced. She had turned her head and lowered it to Dean's shoulder. "Let's get out of here." She had said nervously and was now shaking.

This had caught the alpha-male's attention. He lifted his head quickly and glared at the two of them. The bright red blood dripped from his snout and the carcass had turned the area of snow below pink. He let out a low cautionary growl and lowered his head and continued to eat. Dean instinctively raised his .22 and shot near the pack.

He didn't specifically aim at any coyote, but he did scare them off as he had hoped. He went over to what was left of the dog's body and pulled out a garbage bag.

"Don't come over here honey!" He raised his hand with palm out signaling her not to come over. "We need to return him to the neighbors."

"I know." Ann sobbed. "This is so awful." She watched sheepishly not wanting to go over to the carcass. Ann had no idea that her second encounter with a coyote would be like this. She was grateful for the company of her husband and his rifle.

Dean and Ann had reluctantly headed back towards the house and both pulled the back bag behind them with the dog's body inside. They headed towards their neighbor's, John and Jean's, home which was the house directly next to theirs. Both Ann and Dean were upset and had cried over the loss of the dog. Their own puppies had meant so much to them, how could they possible tell another person what had happened to their dog.

"Wild is wild no matter how beautiful or how cute." Ann sadly said and Dean nodded in reply. They stopped a few feet short of their neighbor's back door and Dean walked up and knocked.

All Things Must End

The Story of Us

Eva drove home, she disappointedly and disgusted turned off the radio in her SUV. The local news story gave the basically disturbing headline of a raided puppy mill on the outskirts of town. This type of news was more worry some to her than the often heard headlines in other parts of the world.

Having been an EMT she was accustom to helping people at their worst moments, and in some of the most awful conditions she had barely batted and eye. A gushing head wound or a broken leg, it was all the same to her. This was something more though; little defenseless dogs and puppies were being boxed in, mistreated, malnourished and not cared for.

"Awful." She muttered to herself and shook her head. She turned her thoughts from the news story to her driveway as she pulled in with quite some difficulty. February in Pennsylvania is not pleasant for driving, let alone shoveling. By mid-afternoon they had four inches on the ground and by the end of the evening they were expecting another eight inches. Her car fish-tailed up the drive. After thirty-one years of her residency in Pennsylvania she should be used to it, but she wasn't.

Eva sighed and placed the shifter in park. She got out and stepped down into the light fluffy snow, walked around to the rear of the vehicle and pulled out a twenty pound bag of puppy food. Carrying the bag she went up the porch steps.

"Another round here we go." She said to herself and opened the door. She was happy to be home even though she loved her job as a vet tech at a local veterinarian hospital. She loved her home, her family, and her two dogs, though often her home life was more of a challenge than work was sometimes. As soon as she stepped in the door she was greeted by the managere' of barks and wagging tails.

She instantly had thought back to day one when the dog's jealousy for each other had begun. The alpha-female had become the beta canine and it was all downhill from there.

Baby Girl, the eldest pup, at eight months old was a beautiful AKC Siberian Husky. She was the queen of her castle. Baby Girl was feminine and had a pristine coat of white and gray mixed. She also had a high-spirited showmanship quality to her. When Eva and her husband Jason first got her she was being sold for fifty dollars from a family located near Pittsburgh, PA who did not want her. The gentleman of the house had told them that he had taken her in when she was born after the next door neighbor had abused her and the other pups. Baby Girl immediately took to their daughter Amber, who was as nine years old. The three of them were smitten by her charm, beauty, and playfulness. So that afternoon a family of three had become a family of four.

In Eva's mind Baby Girl was the antagonist to the current domestic situation, though she could not really blame her entirely for it. Most of the fault was on Eva and Jason. They thought that since she was still a puppy that bringing another puppy into the household would be ok. That was their belief, misconception, and mistake. Baby Girl had ruled alone for five months and didn't want the company of the newest pup, Tazz. He had become her rival and arch nemesis.

Tazz had joined the family two days before Christmas that same year. A local newspaper ad had a spot titled "Free puppies to a good home". Upon calling and visiting the owners the Saunders's were excited that the puppies were German Shepherd and Labrador Retriever mixed.

They admired qualities of the two breeds, a Germador, if you will. This was another case of mistreatment. The seven week old puppies had no vet care and lived in a freezing shed with no heat. The owner's had not cared nor wanted the pups. The choice of which pup was both hard and easy at the same time. Easy, in the respect, that they had a choice of two males and five females, and they knew that they wanted one. The choice was hard that they couldn't take them all; they were all so cute.

A mostly black pup was their first choice. He wasn't timid, despite the freezing temperatures; he came right over to Jason and curled up against his legs. Jason reached down and picked him up. He was shivering and as soon as Jason looked into his big adorable brown eyes that was it. The decision was made. Amber played with a yellow and white female in the corner of the porch and all of the other pups hid underneath a table searching for warmth.

"Hey Amber!" Jason called over "Come check out this little guy."

Both Amber and Eva walked over and almost simultaneously the pair said "Aww". "Can I hold him daddy?" Jason handed her the shivering puppy.

"Just be careful with him." He reminded her.

"I will." She happily replied.

The Saunders's chatted with the family for a bit. All of them were cold as the temperatures continued to rapidly fall in the lower teens. They made their selection. The family giving away the pups didn't want any money, even though the Saunders's offered to pay.

"Are you sure?" Eva asked again to the owner.

"No, it's fine we just want them to go to a good home." The Saunders's thank them again graciously and left with their new puppy.

They were excited and yet saddened that they didn't take another pup. Eva held him on her lap as they drove through the snow covered roads back towards home.

"I can't believe they kept them in that cold shed. If I wasn't so grateful for them giving him to us I would call someone and report it." Jason nodded his head.

Amber bounced around the back seat happily, trying to come up with names for him. The angry emotions passed and the small puppy's shivering had ceased, he was warm and comfortable now with his new family. They drove home in the darkness of the evening. The scenic Christmas lights and decorated houses were all a glow and the family of four had become a family of five.

Once they arrived home Jason had put Baby Girl in Amber's room when they brought the new pup inside. He ran happily around the living room and kitchen. The three of them watched and took turns playing with him. Amber had said excitedly

"It looks like he has a big white 'T' on his chest." Both Jason and Eva noticed this and Eva gave a suggestion.

"He's running around in circles so much, why don't we name his Tazz? Like a Tasmanian Devil?"

"Great idea honey. Tazz it is." Jason replied.

Amber loved the name as well. They all did and they were all happy and excited except for the low growl that could be heard coming from down the hallway.

"I'm home!" Eva bellowed. Jason and Amber were already home watching TV in the living room. Tazz and Baby Girl came running into the kitchen and slid on the tile floor. Jason walked up to Eva, gave her a kiss and took the large bag of dog food from her arms. "Here let me get that for you hun."

"Thanks." She said and returned the kiss.

Eva took off all of her winter gear while the two dogs jumped wildly at the anticipation of being fed. "How were the roads?" Jason asked. "As to be expected, bad as always. I'm glad to be home."

Jason had torn off a corner of the brand new dog food bag and Tazz let out a howl. They all laughed.

"He has such a big attitude." Eva joked. "But he needs to grow into his voice." Jason poured both bowls of food and set them down on opposite sides of the kitchen. It was all downhill from there for the food. Tazz inhaled his food and Baby Girl was surveying hers.

Afterwards both dogs were full and settled and so was the family. Amber went to her book bag and took out a painting that she had done at school and excitedly had shown her mom. Her newest masterpiece.

Amber had talent for drawing and painting and had won some impressive awards from school with her art. She had plaques and trophies from her class, school, and state regional competitions.

"That is a wonderful painting of the woods, Amber. I really love it."

"Thanks mom." She hummed happily to herself and went to her room to hang up her painting.

After dinner the family was relaxed. Just at about the same time when Jason sat down on the couch the two dogs started up again. "Here we go again." He irately said.

Baby Girl had leapt off the love seat, over the coffee table, and landed on Tazz. A loud thud followed by yelps was all that could be heard. By now the Saunders's were used to it; sometimes they found it funny and sometimes not. The two were separated for a bit and the night continued on.

Later that evening another battle was set to begin. A lone toy was placed in the hallway; a trap is set. In the darkness of the adjacent room is the Husky. She is crouched and ready to pounce. The unsuspecting Tazz eyes the toy from afar and runs for it. He leaps, he lands, and he is ambushed. "Gotcha" Baby Girl seems to say with her stance.

Her front legs were lowered and her back legs are raised high. A growling, biting, fur-flying frenzy takes flight down the hallway in a single swooping movement. Then came the body slam.

"Gasps." Were bountiful and the family is amazed by the trap and the execution of the plan. "Baby Girl!" Eva yells.

Baby Girl runs for her crate as she knows she was bad and did wrong. The incident didn't phase Tazz one bit. He walks out of the hallway strutting. He then picks up his toy like a knight claiming his sword. Tazz is victorious in this battle, but the end of the war is still unforeseen. The Saunders's had taken the introduction of the two dogs slow.

However, in the end it didn't matter. If a dog doesn't like another dog, or a person for that matter, there is very little that someone can do to change their mind. Simple bantering play became aggression. Fangs shown, a broken water bowl, and two-ticked off dogs spell disaster for this household. "When will the two of you ever stop?" She looks at Baby Girl, walks by her crate and picks up Tazz, and places him into his crate. She then returned to the couch near Amber and Jason.

She fully intended to enjoy the rest of her evening without the dogs interfering.

"So, how was work today?" Eva asked Jason when she sat back down. Jason worked at the county's Humane Society full-time and as a groomer part-time. He was grooming today.

"Good for the most part. Kinda sad. When I was cleaning this one dog's ears I noticed he had a large round lump in it. After I examined it I brought it to Patricia's attention. She said it looked like a tumor and we took it over to the veterinarian side for an exam and I called the owner. They confirmed it was a tumor. It was really sad. The owner was upset."

Eva listened and looked on with care she set down her cup of blueberry and black tea and asked. "What kind of dog? How old?"

"He's a two year old Border Terrier. Poor thing."

"Must be hard on the family." Eva said and sighed.

A while later Amber let both dogs out of their crates. Tazz took his place next to Jason and Baby Girl took her place next to Eva. Naturally, dogs choose their owners and Eva looked up from her book and glanced at the dogs. She had noticed where each dog went. Each dog was content and Eva, for a moment, envied them. The dogs knew themselves, their likes, dislikes, personalities, and their taste in people for companionship. Many of the attributes she saw in the dogs she also had seen in them individually and respectfully.

The dogs were contented one minute and fighting the next, just like her and Jason. While the dogs had fought most of the time there were also moments where they really loved each other as well.

"I really think they are a lot like us." Eva said and smiled.

"I agree." He replied. At that moment Tazz jumped down off the couch.

"Tazz, where are you going?" Asked Amber.

Baby Girl watched him with raised ears and a peaked interest. *Ding-Ding-Ding!* You could almost hear the bell as Baby Girl leapt off of the couch and onto Tazz again. *Round 17 here we go! Tonight's main event Baby Girl vs. Tazz.* Amber knew better than to keep sitting on the floor. She got up and sat next to her mother. Tonight's victim was the rope toy; a favorite among dogs. Tug-of-War with a twist and the continual hum of a low growl echoed through the living room.

Jason tried to divert the dogs' attention by throwing a ball. This made it worse. Now Tazz was showing his teeth and went after Baby Girl.

"Hey!" Eva yelled and went after Tazz. He was incredibly smart at three months old, but he was still too young for formal obedience training.

Jason and Eva had discussed about teaching the dog's basic obedience commands in German. 'Nune' means

'No' in German. Since Jason was of German heritage and Tazz was a "Germador" it was most fitting to teach the dog some German. The Saunders's loved both dogs and tried not to favor him, but it was hard not to.

The end of the day was upon them. A normal day by any definition, but nothing could have prepared them for tomorrow.

Baby Girl had her one year check-up with the vet. Eva took her and left work early that day. Eva had Baby Girl's leash in hand, when she opened the door Baby Girl trotted in first with her head held high.

"Hello Mrs. Saunders." The receptionist greeted Eva while she signed in.

Eva was a big advocate of pet insurance, and the ASPCA also, so when she saw a jar sitting there on the counter with an ink-jet laser paper printer cover that stated. "Donate to the pets in Haiti Relief." She put a few dollars in the canister then sat down with Baby Girl in the waiting area.

A larger woman appeared in a doorway and called "Baby Girl!" rather loudly. Eva rose and Baby Girl and trotted happily next to her. The exam was usual as always weight taken, eyes, ears, and heart checked. A general check of the spine and legs followed. When the vet got to her paw she found a bump.

The small blackish bump was round and located between the 2nd and 3rd pad on her right rear foot.

"I don't want to alarm you." Said the vet "but it may be a tick."

"A tick!" Eva exclaimed. "She hasn't been outdoors much due to the winter. I don't know where or when she would have gotten a tick on her." The vet, Dr. Ellis, had his assistant retrieve an instrument from a drawer in the exam room and burned the head of the tick off. It made an unpleasant smell, but it did detach and fell off completely.

It took two assistants and Eva to hold Baby Girl down when they removed the tick. The vet assistant took the tick with a pair of tweezers and slipped it gently into a plastic baggie and sealed it.

"We'll have the lab test it right away along with a blood sample from her. You can wait here for the results or we can call you." Said Dr. Ellis.

"I'll wait." Eva replied. She sat down in a chair in the exam room and the waiting and worrying began.

The next forty five minutes dragged on and seemed like an eternity for Eva, but Baby Girl took advantage of the time and slept. Finally the door opened and Dr. Ellis and a vet tech walked in. Dr. Ellis had a somber look in his eyes and his assistant, a tall thin young blonde haired woman, was almost in tears.

"What is it?" Eva asked as she stood up clenching the leash tighter and prepared herself for the worst.

"I'm sorry." He had a saddened look to him now. "She has a tumor in her paw."

Eva took one step back in disbelief. "Oh no!" She exclaimed and could barely believe what she was hearing. "I don't understand Dr. Ellis." Eva hoped there was some type of mistake. "I thought you removed a tick and were checking for Lyme disease?"

"We did test the tick and her blood…" He began to explain as he set his clipboard down. He was a tall, thin, and blonde-haired man He sat on a rolling stool and pushed closer to her as he continued to explain. All she could do is look into his green-tinted eyes and process what she was hearing. "The tick and her blood is negative for the Lyme.

However, when we processed the blood we did a full panel and the tests were conclusive for Osteosarcoma. It is a type of bone cancer found to be common in larger breeds of dogs." Dr. Ellis took an x-ray film and showed Eva that the tumor was located in her foot between her toe and foot bone. When this happens and no one can predict or prevent this. I am sorry." Tears were swelling up in Eva's face and a vet assistant had brought her a glass of water and some handkerchiefs.

Eva leafed through the tests and films, which were being re-run for validity. Everything had happened so quickly she did not even get a chance to call her husband. He was her rock and was stronger than her, now she needed him more than ever. The news was awful and devastating, but she coped with it the best she could. The staff took Baby Girl from the exam room and Eva used her cell phone and almost called Jason. He was at work and had refrained from calling. She wanted so much to cry and confide in him. Animals had held a special place in her heart, and now her heart was breaking. No person, or animal, deserves to go through cancer.

The assistant brought Baby Girl back in the exam room and since it was near the end of the day Eva asked if her and her husband Jason could come in tomorrow for further discussion of Baby Girl's condition. "Of course." Theresa, the vet assistant replied. She gave Eva a warm and sympathetic smile and handed the leash back to Eva. They all exited the room; Eva was leaving with the most horrific news.

Eva could barely drive home. She dreaded telling Jason. How would she break the news to him?

"He'll be home soon." She thought to herself as she glanced to the backseat at her beautiful Baby Girl laying

215

there on the leather seat. She was half asleep with her paws crossed. As she often slept like that dainty and feminine.

The drive home itself was not good. The roads were slick again and though there was not as much snowfall as the day before; it was still enough for her.

"Oh." She said silently to herself and remembered today's date. It was the passing of her maternal grandfather. He would have turned eighty if he was still alive. He had passed from lung cancer and her paternal grandfather had recently passed from prostate cancer. All of these thoughts, along with the day's events, had made her cry. She was tough as could be in the vet's office, but now she had let it all out.

Eva crying had awoken the passenger in the backseat. She edged her head forward and laid it on the armrest of the center console. Eva could only gently pat her on the head and stroked her fur. Hundreds of questions with unknown answers had filled Eva's mind about this dilemma. Out of shear habit she turned on her turn signal and pulled into her driveway.

Jason came home about an hour later. Eva was sitting on the couch with both dogs seated next to her. Eva's face was still pink and red from crying. Amber ran in the living room.

"Hi mom!" She hugged her mother and Eva returned a strong hug.

"Go in your room and play honey." Eva said and tried her best to smile. They would not tell Amber until they knew more. They needed facts and options, and a second opinion first before they told her daughter.

"Ok." Amber replied and went off to her room. Even the dogs were not their usual selves; they weren't bouncing off the walls.

Jason sat down next to Eva and he immediately knew something was wrong. His mind was racing and he held Eva's hand. She hugged him hard and began to explain. "Her exam at the vet's did not go well today…" She hesitated for a second and then continued. I don't know how to say this except for being blunt honey. Baby Girl has cancer."

"What?!" Jason was stunned to say the least. "She's only a year old!" He did his best to process what he just heard.

"The vet found a tick and removed it. They checked her blood and did a full panel. It's Osteosarcoma. The tumor is on her bones of one of her toes and her foot. They did x-rays and showed me all the results.

"Are they sure? Did they redo the tests?" Jason asked in disbelief.

"Yes, they did. We should get a second opinion."

Jason nodded his head at this and said. "Definitely." Eyes closed, leaning on each other, they both of them stroked Baby Girl's fur and cried together.

The news had hit Jason harder than expected. "I don't want her to go through all of that." He swallowed hard and held Eva tighter. Though she did not know him at the time when Jason was seventeen he had a rare form of kidney cancer. The oncologists gave him a five percent chance of survival. He had endured tests, procedures, surgeries, chemo, and radiation, the works. It was the hardest and the most painful experience of his life. "It's going to be hard on all of us…especially her." He said as he continued to pet her.

"We can go together to look over the tests and films. We need to get a second opinion and discuss the options. I want her to be seen by one of the vets that I work with." He heartfeltly said. "I want Dr. Vonburg to take over her care.

Also, since I've been there for a year now I get the discount. It will be helpful. More than anything I've seen how good the vet staff is."

Dr. Vonburg was a senior veterinarian at the pet hospital. She was not boasty or braggy in her skills. To Eva she seemed like a fair and honest woman. Jason admired her never-give-up attitude and her German heritage. Baby Girl would soon be under her care, by far the best vet in the Pittsburgh region. The Verona Valley Veterinarian Hospital had a high standard in excellence and care. They had one of the most prestigious reputations in all of Pennsylvania.

Eva agreed with the decision and she had thought of it already. The Saunders's were a team, strong and unbeatable. They knew Baby Girl was one of them and she would defy the odds.

The next few days came and went, Baby Girl was no different. Her and Tazz continued their antics. For the most part the family had focused on the positive and tried not to let the two dog's fights bother them as much. Amber was told by her parents that Baby Girl was sick and the vet would do everything possible to help her. They gave Amber explanations and kept details to a minimum and only when necessary. The Saunders's were appreciative for their family and little problems became less significant as time went on.

All of the tests and procedures were done again, this time at the Verona Vet Hospital. Everything was repeated including the diagnosis. The dime size tumor was located on Baby Girl's toe bone and a nickel size tumor foot of the same paw. Both were connected to the nerves and muscles. The best case scenario would be a successful surgery, no nerve damage, with minimal side effects and the paw saved. They knew what the worst case scenario was and tried to block the thought from their minds, death. The middle-of-the-road would be a foot amputation and extensive physical therapy. The surgery was scheduled for the end of the week.

Eva and Jason tried to keep life as normal as possible. The few exceptions were more family time and an excess of prayers. Denial for them passed and as the surgery grew near acceptance had started to settle in. They did the best to prepare themselves for the worst, but were still hopeful for the best. At both Eva's and Jason's jobs their co-workers had taken it upon themselves to start a fund and try to raise some extra money to help out with the costs. Even though the discount was a sizeable amount there would still be a balance left over and their friends wanted to help out. The Saunders's were quite avid about volunteering in the community and in return the community had showed them concern and appreciation for their situation.

The day before the surgery they met with a canine physical therapist. Her name was Ashley Sheeter, she was a woman of average height with dark brown mid-length hair. She had a well-known reputation in the Pittsburgh area for canine rehabilitation. The idea of a doggy wheel-chair was brought up in the meeting, but it was tabled and will only be used as a last resort. "Dr. Vonburg and I have been consulting on your dog's case and I feel that as long as the surgery is successful Baby Girl will make a full recovery."

Both Jason and Eva smiled at the thought and their optimism remained high.

"But please know. I can only do what I can." Sheeter said cautiously. She never wanted to give owners false hope, yet she did want hope to prevail. "I'm going to go get some pamphlets for you about canine physical therapy. You should read up on it." Sheeter exited the room and Jason and Eva held each other. The sun shown in through the window; it had shown brighter than it had in weeks. The snow had subsided and temperatures were rising that day. Hope was plentiful.

A few minutes later Sheeter had returned with the pamphlets along with a vet assistant, Tracey. "Here Mr. and Mrs. Saunders I have some pre-op paperwork and instructions to give you." Eva signed and initialed the forms. Baby Girl sat at their feet; she wagged her tail with her tongue hanging out and smiled in her own way as well. Eva was aware of all the pre-surgery formalities having to perform the same duties at her work, but now she was on the opposite side. She did not like it and hope she would never have to be on that side of things again.

That night the family took comfort in each other's company. "Can I have another piece of pizza dad?" Amber asked.

"Sure." Jason replied. Amber reached across the table and took another slice. They rented new releases, ate pizza, and played with their pups. Each dog was given a special treat that day – pig ears and cow hoofs. Favorites among dogs.

Since Baby Girl was not allowed water after a certain time that night and the notion of licking a pig ear was most pleasing to her. Spending time together was exactly what the family needed.

Baby Girl was outwardly fine. She no longer limped from the biopsy or required medication. Besides what was growing in her paw, she was in excellent health. Inside she knew the family's behavior had changed. They family had suspected all of this and knew it to be true, mostly for the positive.

By nightfall Amber had gotten ready for bed and asked "Can Baby Girl sleep in my room tonight?" It was most appropriate and Jason and Eva were pleased. Baby Girl trotted along behind Amber and Eva tucked the both of them in. Amber was young but loved her dogs more than anything. They were her best friends and companions. Baby Girl laid on the bed as well at Amber's feet. When Eva exited the room she closed the door and heard Amber's prayer asking for Baby Girl to be ok and get better soon. She asked God to help her mom and dad take care of Baby Girl and said that she loved her a lot. Then Eva heard her little daughter's "Amen" at the end and it touched her heart more than she ever thought possible and it brought tears to her eyes.

Soon the house was quiet and Eva lay in bed and thought about that night. She was comforted by the thought that the dogs did not fight tonight. To her it was a positive sign. Jason crawled in bed and held her. He kissed her and whispered in her ear "I love you." He kissed her again and they fell asleep.

Their SUV pulled in the hospital parking lot an hour before the surgery, as instructed. The minimal warmth of the day before was long forgotten and this day brought frigid temps in the teens.

"Here we go." Jason said as he put the vehicle in park. Baby Girl looked up in the front seat with her tail thumping against the seat before they exited the vehicle.

Upon entering the building they were greeted by most of the staff that was on duty that day. There were numerous smiles and the occasional hug exchanged. Jason signed them in and Vanessa, a vet tech, had taken Baby Girl back to a prep area. The two Saunders's took a seat in the waiting area. They had already said their good bye's to Baby Girl this morning before leaving the house.

Soon they were lead into an exam room. "Good morning." Dr. Vonburg said as she came in the room.

"We followed the pre-op instructions. I felt guilty eating breakfast this morning." Eva said.

"It's alright. Most owners feel the same way." Replied Vonburg. "The surgery should take about two hours or so as you know. You can wait in here or the waiting room, whichever you prefer."

"We'll be in the front waiting room." Jason answered.

"Don't worry. We'll take good care of her." Dr. Vonburg said as she put a hand on Jason's shoulder.

"Thank you." Said Eva and they all exited the room.

Waiting was the worst part of it all. Only a week had passed since the discovery of the cancer and here they are already. Time that week flew by, but now time seemed to stop while they waited. Thinking back, Eva recalled the scuffles between the two dogs. Would Tazz miss her if she didn't come home with them? How would Amber deal with it? Eva had to put dogs to sleep in the past and so had Jason. It was a difficult thing to do and she prayed she would not have to do that now.

Tracey approached and sat down next to them. "I thought we'd, meaning the staff, would let you know that the collection of donations for Baby Girl's surgery had a high response. In total so far all the locations together raised about fifteen hundred dollars."

"Wow, really?!" Eva's eyes had filled with tears as she took in the good news.

"Thank you for letting us know. That is wonderful that so many people had donated!" Jason said with vivid excitement.

"We are so grateful for everything." Eva had told Tracey and Tracey in turn replied. "She will pull through it."

222

Eva was thankful for all the staff's compassion and though she did not work there she felt close to them from this unfortunate event. Tears fell from Eva's eyes and she leaned in closer to Jason; holding him tight. He held her and they both prayed silently.

Another hour passed and Tracey reappeared. "She's out of surgery and in recovery now. Let's go back to a room so the doctor can go over the results of the surgery with you.

"Das ist ja toll!" Dr. Vonburg exclaimed happily when Jason and Eva walked into the room. Eva was taken back, she had no idea what that meant. Jason smiled. With his German heritage and comprehension for the language he knew exactly what she meant. He clasped his hands and leaned towards Eva and quickly said. "It means 'This is great!'." Eva enthusiastically exhaled and walked over to hug the German doctor.

"Wait. Please." Italia Vonburg had held up her hand palm forward in a stopping type of motion. Though the news was good, it was not great and she attempted to ward off any premature celebrations. Eva had a raised brow expression and pulled back a bit confused.

"Is everything all right?" Panic stuck Eva. "I thought she pulled through ok." Eva tried to understand exactly what Dr. Vonburg was saying. "She did survive, but not everything went as well as planned. The tumor was attached to the nerve and muscles, as you knew. I tried to separate the tumor and leave minimal damage to the nerve or muscles, but it was not possible. I'm sorry, but we had to amputate her foot." Both Jason and Eva were taken back and surprised to say the least. They were both relieved and dismayed at the same time.

The doctor continued. "Also, with the amputation we had stopped any risk of the cancer spreading up the leg or to other parts of her body." Jason nodded in acceptance of what she was saying as she continued. "After Baby Girl heals then Ms. Sheeter will take over her care with the physical therapy. Baby Girl and the entire family will have to adjust to the physical changes, but overall all her prognosis is now good. It's a miracle that Baby Girl did so well."

Eva and Jason knew this to be true. Eva continued to be teary, but now the tears were of joy and not of loss. Eva completed the hug with Italia Vonburg, who reciprocated now.

"Thank you for everything doctor." Jason said. The Saunders's got to briefly visit with Baby Girl in recovery and were told that they could bring her home in a few days. She was sedated and resting.

In the lobby smiles and handshakes went all around. The staff was thanked fully by Jason and Eva and their baby girl was left in their care. They were overjoyed. Jason and Eva left pulling away in their SUV through the bright sunny day. Their hearts were full. The number five still reigned, all family members were present and accounted for. The drive home was peaceful and Eva could not wait to tell Amber the good news.

The next few months were a challenging transition for all the Saunders's. Baby Girl adjusted quite well physically and her spirit was unbreakable. Tazz won a few extra battles, yet the war was ongoing. The two dogs over time even started to like each other. Who would have figured?

Amber played with both of them every chance she got with no objections from her parents. Family is family no matter what despite the size of one's paw.

A Change of Pace

For the last ten years of my career I have worked in the medical field. A hospital, chemo facility, and physician office have been my top three entries on my resume. Professionalism has been a large part of my life and still currently is, just in another setting.

Changing careers is difficult from a nine to five full-time typical desk job to a part-time rush-until-you-drop job. All my life I have been taught that money comes first and family comes second, though people and family tell you different, that is the truth.

Work comes first. Well, I don't agree with that philosophy anymore. For me it became a matter of leaving my daughter in a day camp over the summer for eleven hours per day five days a week versus three days per week only six hours a day. The later was harder on the budget, but better for our family.

For me it became a notion of "If we only have one life to live and our children should be the most important aspect of our life then why should I put money first and be stagnant behind a desk?"

I traded in my business-casual attire for a pair of light purple scrubs covered black and white paw prints. Being in my thirties it was a vast career switch, but an exciting one. I love dogs and the idea of being a groomer and the whole beautification idea of taking a dog, bathing, drying, and clipping until he/she shines and looks spectacular is a rush for me.

I know when I take my own dogs to the groomers I love picking them up. The experience is wonderful for an owner. Your canine smells superb, looks fabulous, and dons an exquisite bandana or bow. It's like you have a new and improved dog compared to the one that you brought in. Though I only know a little about grooming and some aspects of it seem intimidating, especially cats, I love it and am very excited and happy to be working at the grooming salon.

My previous work environment, aka the "desk job", had been doing medical insurance billing. I did enjoy most of the work, but it came with a price. I was often yelled at and cursed by the patients whom did not have any insurance. Unfortunately, this was part of the job and my worst patients had been the ones from Trenton, NJ. I was told off in several languages. My new job at the grooming salon is pleasing more often than not. Occasionally an upset client may speak his/her opinion but for the most part it is not directed at me or anything that I had done. The atmosphere is very different and very much to my liking.

I recall my interview with Patrice, the grooming manager. She is a very fair and distinct woman. The "interview" was the most informal, yet informative, one that I had ever had. I presented my resume, filled out an application, and was escorted back to the grooming area. Patrice spoke to me a little about the job while scanning my resume as she was brushing a miniature collie. She was quite good at multi-tasking and in the forty-five minutes that I was at the grooming salon there were two emergencies to deal with along with the full schedule of dogs. Patrice handled everything like a charm. I knew when to patiently wait and stay out of the way and when there was a break in the chaos we talked.

Jason had been working there for six months and seen Patrice interview a lot of people. He knew her signals, good and bad, when it came to interviewing and hiring. At one point when Patrice was busy I used the restroom and she had pulled Jason aside and told him that she really liked me,

which was a big plus. I got a call from Patrice two days later
and I had a "working interview". Jason was an assistant
groomer, but I needed time and training to work my way up.
I started the next day and I was mostly excited, but a tad
nervous also. I wanted to be as professional as I could and do
a good job.

Day 1: Training as the Salon and Day Spa Receptionist

Jason and I went to work at the same time and he
started his day working as the pet bather and grooming
assistant while I trained at the reception desk with Marie, the
current receptionist. A flurry of emotions clouded my mind
during the course of the day. I was nervous, excited,
intimidated, and thrilled; it was a learning experience. I got to
check-in clients and bring the dogs into the grooming area
and secure them in a kennel. Next was the paperwork – lots
of it. The phones and computer software were the easiest to
handle. Then there were the check-out processes and
payment processing.

All in all the day was ok. There were as many
positives as negatives and through the day and during the lull
times I got to fold the cute bandanas and make treat bags for
the pampered pooches.

With any new job there is training. By the time I left I
had a headache of gigantic proportions. It must have been
from absorbing so much information in a small amount of
time. I was there a total of six hours, which flew by.

Marie is very good at training. She is the full-time
receptionist whom has worked there for the last fourteen
years. She is in her mid-sixties and has talked about retiring
soon. There is one other part-time receptionist and some of

the grooming assistants rotate in as needed. Two days a week isn't much, but it helps.

The most memorable part of the day was the dogs themselves. There was a Golden Retriever, two yellow labs, a Westie, two Cocker Spaniels, and a Shih Tzu. It was a pretty light day, yet I can't imagine how an extremely busy day of thirty to forty dogs would work? I'm sure some day I will find out.

The job is so much different from what I am used to. Patrice has proved to be difficult to work with as she is very meticulous, but *Hey it's only my first day* I have told myself and day 1's "working interview" went well. So, now I was invited for another working interview – day 2. Whew! Here I come.

Touch My Heart

Jason and I have seen all sorts of mistreatment of animals in all types of deplorable conditions and have encountered all types of animals in the wild. This was by far the worst yet as far as a wild animal goes.

We were driving to our favorite fishing spot. It was a late May sunny afternoon with Memorial Day all-too-fastly approaching. Jason drove and we passed under the canopy of newly budding leaves on the large oak, maple, and poplar trees. They had blocked most of the rays yet the sun was still strong and penetrating through. Tazz seemed thankful that he was able to tag along with us and hung his head out the window with tongue flapping in the wind.

We approached a black Cadillac with a small fishing boat in tow who flagged us down and asked for directions. We were glad to oblige him and the route to the nearest major road was a simple "left, left, and a right turns". The mid-fifties man had thanked us profusely while Tazz continued to bark his head off and we kept driving towards Neely's Point, a favorite for locals for on-shore fishing.

The asphalt road ended and gave way to a dirt road and now the sunlight was not able to shine through those oaks; it was nice and shady. We were five minutes away from the fishing spot when Jason and I simultaneously spotted a small lanky animal walking in the middle of the dirt roadway. At first I thought it was a medium-sized coyote walking, it was not. As we drove a little closer I noticed it was a very small fawn as did Tazz; the bursting of growling and barking rose from the backseat.

"Oh poor thing must be lost." I said to Jason whom was just as concerned I was about the fawn. Jason pulled up on the side of the road and placed the car in park.

"I'm going to go check on it." Jason said to me as I kept watching the lost animal. "Go in the back of the car and bring my gun up front just incase mommy deer decides to show up. I don't want to take any chances." I nodded and headed for the rear hatch while Jason started walking towards the animal.

I was concerned for the animal but still was anxious about its wild parents. I slid the gun case in the front passenger seat and got into the drivers seat. Having Tazz there was a relief he was very protective and the barking would hopefully deter any animals. Inching up forward slowly I thought perhaps the fawn was injured or lost. It knew Jason was near it and it did not take off running as most animals do. Amber was in the backseat. She picking stickers off of her newest Disney sticker book and only occasionally glanced up to see what was going on.

I continued to glide slowly forward with my foot riding the brake. The next thing I saw made me feel uneasy. *What in the world is he doing?* I thought when he reached down and petted the fawn. I put the car in park and just watched him for a minute and looked up at Amber every now and then while Tazz growled low and continually. Jason stood for a few minutes and kept petting him.

I sat there looking forward and saw the fawn's fur was a little matted. The spots were there of course and guessing the age I thought maybe it was two weeks old or so. Twice it turned its head and the face looked to be an odd shape and dark colored, which is not typical. Jason rose up and walked back. I started to open the door to get out and see if I could help or do anything.

Out of the car now my face met Jason's and I was instantly concerned. He was crying and upset as I had ever seen him; his face was red and swelled with tears. Immediately I knew something was wrong with the fawn.

"Honey what's wrong?" I asked with concern and uneasiness. He could barely get the words out as he approached and stopped.

"It doesn't have a face." He came around the back of the car and sat for a minute crying uncontrollably. He then continued. "Its nose, mouth, and one eye are completely gone. Ripped off and bleeding." I gasped and was horrified. I knew it acted oddly and from about twenty feet away I could not see its face up close, but I never would have thought of that.

Jason had momentarily stopped and regained is composure. "Eva I have to put it down. It's bleeding a lot. I don't know if it was attacked by another animal, but there's no mouth or nose left. It keeps screeching in pain and I have to do something." Now I had started crying. I knew putting it down was for the best. No one could do anything for this animal, it was going to die and suffer and that was last thing either of us wanted for it. I went back to the front seat and talked to Amber whom now was alert to us crying and was asking about the fawn. Jason had gotten the gun out of the front seat and walked towards the baby deer.

During our conversation the fawn had stayed close to the road but wandered forward just around the bend and when it walked it had looked like it was given a sleeping pill, being wobbly and disoriented. Jason and the fawn were out of eyesight from the car. This was agreeable to me as I did not want Amber to see what was coming. I calmed Tazz down and spoke to Amber.

"Amber, the fawn is hurt really really bad and is going to die."

"Oh no!" Her blue eyes swelled up and she began to protest.

"Since no one can help the fawn and its suffering daddy is going to take care of it. It's not right to leave it." I heard the first shot while Amber was talking and now Tazz went crazy. To him a gunshot meant hunting and he wanted to be near Jason. Several more shots went off and I seen Jason lift up the small frail lifeless body across the street and lay it in the weeds. He stood there for a minute and I pulled up next to him.

I was confident that Amber did not see nor pay attention to the gunshots since Tazz went nuts in the car and Amber was distracted. I felt some relieve when it was over, but I knew how hard it was for Jason to do right thing. He walked back to the front passenger seat and got in with head lowered and quietly crying. "Are you ok?" I regretfully asked. I knew he wasn't, but that's what people do ask if you are ok in the worst situations when clearly someone is not.

He looked up at me and I began crying again along with him. I gave him a kiss and a long strong hug while we sat on side of the deserted dirt road. Tazz was trying to jump in the front seat, but was blocked and was only able to set his two front paws on the armrest. He stood as tall as he possibly could and licked Jason's tears off his face. This made him smile and cry more simultaneously.

"Do you want to go home?" I asked.

"No. We can still go." He replied and tried to regain some pride, but his pride was gone. This had traumatized him to where the events rapidly and uncontrollably replayed in his head for hours and the nightmares lasted for days.

So we went fishing. For most of the duration we didn't speak about it in attempt to come to terms with what happened and for the most part it worked. At one point Jason was sitting in out red camping chair with Tazz faithfully sitting next to him and Jason reached down and stroked the fur on Tazz's middle back. It was upsetting and reminded him of the fawn's fur. It was soft yet brittle. Jason knelt down and held Tazz and let it all out. He was not only crying because of what had happened to the fawn and what he had done to the fawn as well, but he sobbed for Tazz.

He loves Tazz more than any other dog, pet, or animal. Jason had told me that when he first saw the fawn's face he turned his head and looked up at him with his only eye. Jason could only describe the feeling as if he were shot in the heart. He loved this fawn if even though it was only in his life for a few minutes. The look that the fawn gave him so much reminds him of how Tazz looks at him.

Jason can look into Tazz's eyes and see that there is so much more in there than just a dog. He is a companion that loves him unconditionally. Dusk came, the full moon showed it's self in all its brightness and we packed up and left for the night, no fish caught. It was quite a disappointing night and not because of the lack of bites. On the way back Tazz laid on Amber's lap and Jason and I talked about the night's events. He kept questioning if he did the right thing and I did my best to reassure him that he did.

We pondered what type of animal may have done that: wolf, coyote, bear, or mountain lion. It was an awful sight and our hearts went out to that little fawn. We both knew how much this experience changed our lives and in acceptance we both tried to come to terms with it the best we could.

To me, with my views on life, is that everything happens for a reason. I think that we were meant to be there at that time and come across that fawn on the dirt road. He needed help and I think that is perhaps one of the reasons why he did not run off. He needed help to end his suffering and Jason was the person who was able to do it. I give him a lot of credit. If I was there by myself I would not have been able to do it and would have taken the situation so much harder than he did. We rest in the fact knowing that we did the right thing. In life it always seems that the doing the right thing is always the hardest of the choices we make.

The little fawn will remain in our thoughts and our hearts.

One Jealous Pup

Baby Girl's jealously of Tazz continued for a year and beyond. They did get along somewhat and at times they were caring and playful with each other. However, sometimes you need to decide if two dogs are more than you can handle, and this was the case for us. Tazz had grown to be large quicker than what Jason and I thought and he was a handful. When it came to excessive fighting, barking, and growling baby Girl had exceeded the limit. Tazz took it all in stride, while she did not.

Baby Girl's jealously led to a steady flow of broken and damaged items in our house. Chewing and some wear and tear is to be expected, but when chairs are constantly flipped over and couches ripped then something needs to be done. Broken end tables and ripped bed mattresses were also a few of the casualties found around our home. In no time flat the house would be clean and quite and the next it was a level four disaster area.

Tazz was Jason's pride and joy. I loved big dogs, and especially labs. I guess Baby Girl knew that. We played with Baby Girl as much as we played with Tazz to avoid jealousy for one and also because we loved both dogs. Though Jason had made no effort to hide that Tazz was his favorite. Tazz and Jason would play with a rope toy doing tug-of-war and Baby Girl would run up with another toy in her mouth and growled a series of "look at me growls". She had not been happy for a while, since after the time when she was the first and only canine in the house. Things had changed and now Jason and I both thought that Baby Girl would be happier with another family.

Plans are made, but no one ever knows how things are going to work out. We already had Baby Girl and decided to take Tazz in when he was a puppy. It didn't work out like we planned. I guess when it comes to dogs sometimes I feel more of an "intermediate" dog owner and an actual dog owner. This was the case of my first two dogs: Rocky and Angel. Rocky was a shelter dog and Angel was neglected and abused. Both dogs went on to find permanent homes. This was now the situation with Baby Girl. She was abused as a pup and passed around from neighbor to neighbor who didn't want her so we took her in.

She has come a long way since she first came to live with us. In many ways I am proud of her. Firstly, she doesn't act like a cat anymore. She likes to play ball and fetch and catch objects in mid-air. Second, she's trustworthy and beautiful. She often, for the last six months, slept on Amber's bed. She was very caring and affectionate to us. And lastly, she filled out hearts with love, peace, and respect for her and each other. I often envy how dog's live. They don't have the complex problems and emotions that their owner's have. They know when you are sad and when you are happy.

It was heart-warming to find her a good family. The first woman whom answered the ad and came to see Baby Girl didn't even make it through the kitchen. As soon as I opened the door she felt the need to skip all formalities and demanded to see her papers and asking for proof of her purebred status. It was good for her that the weather wasn't bad, because the only thing she did was wasting her time by driving here from Pittsburgh. I remember thinking I hope I could find a decent family to adopt her. This woman with the short red hair whom held the snake-skin handbag and drove the Lincoln Towncar was not it. Sorry, look for a breeder next time lady.

Family number two were the Bakers. They were much nicer first off and the lack of attitude was a good start. They were a young family, a couple in their late twenties with a four-year old boy; they were Mike, Kim, and Robbie. The introduction went well for all of us. Tazz was thankfully locked in the bedroom and only escaped once and at least no harm was done. Baby Girl, being her affectionate self, loved the three of them and took to them magnificently. She cuddled and played and loved it when they petted her. It's like she knew what was going on and turned her charm on full blast to the perspective family.

Baby Girl has always liked men better and women and kids the best. Robbie had gotten the most attention from her, Mike was second, but he also got a lot of kisses, and Kim was third. Yep, dogs choose their people. The most hopeful and thankful thing about the Baker's was the fact that they did not have any other dogs or cats. Kim's family, mother and brother, both raise and breed Huskies. She was interested in the fact that she was a purebred, and looked at her papers and vet records, but was not pushy or bitchy about it. I suspect that they may decide to breed Baby Girl in the future, but as long as they treat her right and give her a good home then that is ok with me. She would have beautiful offspring.

Jason, Amber, and I all liked the Baker's and had a good feeling about them. After a forthy-five minute introduction and meeting it was decided mutually that Baby Girl had her new family. Upon looking at the papers it caught Mike's attention that her original name was Sasha, it was the name that she was registered under and born with. The three of them liked that name better than Baby Girl. Each of us took our turns saying a quick goodbye to Baby Girl, but Amber had the most touching goodbye of all. She hugged and squeezed her for a minute and kissed the top of her head.

"I love you and have fun with your new family." I almost cried, but held it until after they left. Jason had escorted the Baker's outside with Baby Girl to their car.

It was official she was adopted, leaving our home to go to theirs. Baby Girl Saunders was now Sasha Baker. Like any responsible pet owner I contacted the new owners, Mike and Kim, a few days later to see how everyone was adjusting. They were all doing well and Robbie loved playing with her in the backyard; they were teaching her how to play Frisbee. It was a win-win situation for everyone involved. Baby Girl got the best possible home with no other pets and a loving family. She was an affectionate, adorable, beautiful girl who came to own the right family.

Bye Baby Girl – you will be missed.

Time to Say Goodbye

It is a fact of life, what lives dies and nothing stays the same, everything eventually changes. It's in these moments of loss when one knows what is truly important in their life. The loss of a pet can be just as hard as the loss of a loved one, as some pets are an extension of their family.

I've had to deal with the loss of my first dog, Samantha. She had lived for twelve years when she passed and she had lived a full live for a dog. Jason has had to deal with the loss of Milo, his first dog as well. Milo was walking along the wooded border of their property when a hunter had mistaken Milo for game and shot him.

Sometimes the most painful of all goodbyes are not the death of a pet, but the separation from the living ones. These are the canines that eternally touch our hearts. Often there are unexplained and un-understandable circumstances of life and a life-altering change occurs. Some of us are forced to make hard choices to give up our companions to another person, *or even worse a shelter*.

When I say "or even worse a shelter" I am referring to the fact that the previous owners of the pets are not allowed to know where their four-legged companion has gone to. For some fortunate persons a family member or friend can take in their dog, but when your dog goes to a shelter that is not the case. You walk in, fill out a form, answer a few questions, and turn over the leash with your best friend attached at the other end. Your dog is taken in, evaluated, and in the end becomes a part of someone else's home.

Adopting a dog is an exciting experience except if you are the one who makes the hard choice to give up the animal in the first place.

I know regretfully about this heart-tearing feeling just as well as anyone else who has experienced it. This was the case with my Rocky and Angel. They were like my children and an extension of my family. An ended first marriage meant a move from a house to an apartment which in turn meant "no dogs". The choice to take both of them to the Humane Society was heavy-hearted yet necessary. The responsible action is often the one that hurts the most. Even though one may feel stricken with grief life does go on.

If our dogs could stay with us and live as long as the average person does they would be the wisest animals in the world. Dogs know us better than we know ourselves and complete us more than we realize. The short-lived spurt in which they co-exist, co-habitate, and co-inspire us just does not seem like enough. They touch our lives and our hearts endlessly, whether it's for a day or a lifetime.

Acceptance (A Poem)

I am a dog,
I can be brash and born in all places.
Refrain from the lash,
Naturally we are crutches and braces.

Whether calm and collected or fierce and fighting,
Give no remorse and accept no pity when docile or
biting.
I'm here through it all from a crystal clear dusk to the
morn sunny warm dawn,
You are the doe and I am the fawn.

I grow and spread and reach and sing,
As you take me under your wing.
Through fetch and play or comfort and sorrow,
I will always be there - now, then, and tomorrow.

Bibliographies, Quotes, and References

Book Bibliographies and Quotes

Paws & Effect The Healing Power of Dogs. Sharon Sakson. 2007. Alyson Books. New York, NY.

"The human-canine bond, as we see it today, is the modern manifestation of an even that scientists say occurred more than ten thousand years ago, the domestication of the wild canine." Pg. 9.

A Dog Named Christmas. Greg Kincaid. 2008. The Doubleday Publishing Group. New York, NY.

"We had a freedom of few that are brave enough to own." Pg. 3.

Animals in Translation – Using the Mysteries of Autism to Decode Animal Behavior. Temple Grandin and Catherine Johnson. 2005. Scribner. New York, NY.

"Animals love other animals." Pg. 109

"There are some animals who, like some people, have a form of genius." Pg. 287.

The Illustrated Encyclopedia of Dog Breeds. Joan Palmer. 1994. The Wellfleet Press. Edison, NJ. -no quotes, only reference

Great Danes Today. Di Johnson. 1994. Howell Book House. New York, NY. Pgs. 29 – 41. – no quotes, only reference

How Dogs Learn. Mary R. Burch, Ph. D. and Jon S. Bailey, Ph. D. 1999. Howell Book House, New York, NY. Pgs. 3 – 7, 10, 15, 20, 27 – 30.

Hunting Dog Know-How. David Michael Duffy. 1965. Van Nostrand Reinhold Company. New York, NY 6, 8, 20-21, 52

Saved!. M.L. Papurt, DVM. 1997. Barron's Educational Series, Inc., Hauppauge, NY. Pgs. 20 – 27, 53-55, 58, 62-63.

The Iams Company Complete Dog Owner's Manual. Amy Marder, Debra Horwitz, Lynn Cole. 1997. Fog City Press. San Francisco, CA. Pgs. 50 – 51, 143 – 145

The New Complete Saint Bernard. 1966. Milo Denlinger, Professor Albert Heim, Mrs. Henry H. Hubble. Et. Al. Howell Book House Inc., New York, NY. Pgs. 11-12, 17-18, 20-22.

Man's Best Friend. National Geographic Book of Dogs. 1966. revised edition. Editor Melville Bell Grosvenor. Publisher. R.R. Donnelley and Sons Company. Chicago, IL. Pgs. 71, 215, 251-253, 288-289, 324 – 325, 327.

Training You To Train Your Dog. New Revised Edition. Blanche Saunders. 1965. Doubleday and Company, Inc. Garden City, NJ. Pgs. 86 – 89.

Mondo Canine. Jon Winokur. 1991. Penguin Books USA Inc., New York, NY.
Pg 76 – photo of pooch in sidecare. From the Bettmann Archive.

The Encyclopedia of the Dog. Fogle, Bruce DVM. 1995. DK Publishing, Inc. New York, NY. Pg. 179

Online

The American Society for the Prevention of Cruelty to Animals (ASPCA), <http://www.aspca.org>

American Kennel Club, <http://www.akc.org>

Continental Kennel Club, <http://www.continentalkennelclub.com>

VPI Pet Insurance, <http://www.petinsurance.com>

World Small Animal Veterinary Association, <http://www.wsava.org>

Journal of American Veterinary Medical Association, <http://avmajournals.avma.org/loi/javma>

Rasmusen, Jan. "Vaccinating Small Dogs: Risks Vets Aren't Revealing." 30 Sept. 2009. <http://www.dogs4dogs.com>

Veterinary & Aquatic Services Department, Drs. Foster & Smith. "Osteosarcoma (Bone Cancer) in Dogs." <http://www.peteducation.com/article.cfm>

Tesumethanon, Veera, DVM, et al. "Clinical Diagnosis for Rabies in Live Dogs." <http://www.dog-health-guide.org/dogbiterabies.html>

Stregowski, Jenna, RVT. "Rabies and Your Dog." <http://dogs.about.com/bio/Jenna-Stregowski-RVT-43548.htm>

Centers for Disease Control and Prevention <http://www.cdc.gov/rabies/about.html>

Food and Drug Administration. "Melamine Pet Food Recall of 2007" <http://www.fda.gov/AnimalVeterinary/SafetyHealth/RecallsWithdrawals/ucm129575.htm>

FDA's Consumer Health Information Web page_1. 19 February 2008. <http://www.fda.gov/ForConsumers/ConsumerUpdates/default.htm>

Food and Drug Administration <http://www.fda.gov/Safety/Recalls/ArchiveRecalls/2007/ucm112172.html>

About the Author...

I live in Erie, Pennsylvania with my family, close to my friends and extended family, which are a big part of my life. I have spent the first thirty-four years of my life in western Pennsylvania. I love the atmosphere of the region from the cities to the mountains. I find myself most comfortable with the familiar and often am caught off-guard by the unexpected.

Having said that, my dogs keep me off-guard as much as they possibly can and being the owner of several dogs, mostly large breeds, I am always up for a challenge. I have also been a part of a professional K-9 search and rescue group for four years and an EMT volunteer for six years adds to the experience of being prepared and learning to expect the unexpected. Dogs have played an important role in my life, this is why I started writing and from where I draw my inspiration. I teach my dogs and in return I learn more than they do.

Learning in life is a continual process which extends beyond high school and post-secondary education. My education has consisted of an Accounting degree and Computer Science diploma (Tri-State Business Institute) as well as Sociology studies at Edinboro University of Pennsylvania. The personal attainment of social academics is to have open-mindedness regarding our society. By profession I am a medical billing specialist and have worked in the medical field for the last fifteen years, but at heart I love to read, write, and learn. I strive to convey my writing towards social issues and their effects on everyday normal people, the contributors in society, you! Thank you to my family and friends.

www.ingramcontent.com/pod-product-compliance
Lightning Source LLC
Chambersburg PA
CBHW071955040426

42447CB00009B/1341